TERRIFIC
CHICKEN

Chicken Véronique, page 24

TERRIFIC
CHICKEN

RODALE

© 2004 by Rodale Inc.

Printed in the United States of America
Rodale Inc. makes every effort to use acid-free ∞, recycled paper ♻.

Cover photograph: Mitch Mandel
Cover recipe: Chicken, Broccoli, & Pineapple Stir-fry,
        Courtesy of Dole Food Company, page 48
Food stylist: Melissa DeMayo
Illustrations: Judy Newhouse

Produced by:
BETH ALLEN ASSOCIATES, INC.

President/Owner: Beth Allen
Designer: Monica Elias
Art Production Director: Laura Smyth (smythtype)
Culinary Consultant/Food Editor: Deborah Mintcheff
Food Writer: Jean Galton
Copy Editor: Brenda Goldberg
Public Relations Consultants: Stephanie Avidon, Melissa Moritz
Nutritionist: Michele C. Fisher, Ph.D., R.D.

Library of Congress Cataloging-in-Publication Data

Terrific chicken.
    p.   cm.
  Includes index.
  ISBN 1–57954–950–0 hardcover, tqc
  ISBN 1–59486–060–2 hardcover, qtf
  1. Cookery (Chicken) 2. Quick and easy cookery.
TX750.5.C45T47 2004
641.6'65–dc22   2003022751

  4 6 8 10 9 7 5 3   hardcover, tqc
2 4 6 8 10 9 7 5 3 1 hardcover, qtf

RODALE

WE INSPIRE AND ENABLE PEOPLE TO IMPROVE
THEIR LIVES AND THE WORLD AROUND THEM

FOR MORE OF OUR PRODUCTS
WWW.RODALESTORE.COM
(800) 848-4735

CONTENTS

INTRODUCTION

How do you handle rush hour?

Not the rush hour when you're stuck in traffic—the real rush hour that starts after you come home after another day when there's only a few minutes left before suppertime. Well if there's a package of chicken in the refrigerator, you're in luck because right now you hold in your hands over 100 solutions to your rush-hour dilemma. It's *Terrific Chicken*—a cookbook we've created just for you.

Thumb through this collection of 100 of our favorite chicken recipes. You're likely to find a great fast solution to tonight's supper by checking out the super-fast recipes (just look for all those labeled SuperQuick). Choose the Chicken Schnitzel with Lemon (page 98), and you'll be in and out of the kitchen in 15 minutes flat. Or the Mediterranean Chicken Breasts (page 34) with a cheesy crumb crust...or Chicken with Dijon Crème (page 37) with a French touch. Every SuperQuick recipe goes from "shopping bag to table" in 30 minutes or less, juicier and tastier than you ever thought possible.

For a fast bite another night, toss up Chicken Waldorf Salad (page 42). It "goes elegant" with a creamy yogurt dressing sauce you can whisk up in just 5 minutes. On a night when there's a little extra time, invite a few friends over, and fire up the grill. Cook up some spicy North Carolina Barbecue (page 103), making sure to slather on plenty of the thick and tangy sauce, so it goes to the table dripping with juices every time.

You'll quickly see that *Terrific Chicken* is much more than just another recipe book. It's filled with fresh ideas, as well as practical, tried-and-true advice you'll turn to often. Start off by reading the next chapter, "Fresh Ideas with Chicken." You'll find six exciting techniques for working with chicken...one even shows you how (and why) to cook it under a brick! Each of the sensational ways takes little time, offers the scientific "why it works," and ends up letting you serve tastier, juicier chicken than you have ever thought possible.

But that's just the beginning. We've teamed up with test kitchens of famous food manufacturers and other cooking pros from coast to coast—with one goal in mind: to bring you 100 fabulous, fast, flavor-packed recipes. You'll discover that they're all quick and easy...they use fewer ingredients than you might be used to but never skimp on taste. All come kitchen tested to ensure perfect results every time, even if you're just learning how to cook. Some even come with On the Menu ideas to help you plan what's for dinner, whatever the occasion, weekday or weekend, however little time you have.

Throughout this book, you'll find Cooking Basics sidebars that reveal simple time-saving secrets. For instance, learn all about *spatchcocking* (that's just a fancy word for butterflying), which lets you roast a whole chicken that's crispy golden on the outside, full of moistness and flavor on the inside—in half the time.

But that's not all. You'll also find first-hand advice in our Cook-to-Cook boxes that share quick-cooking tips from cooks just like you. You'll see tips for saving time by Microwaving in Minutes to precook chicken before grilling it. Take a peek into our new chicken case (page 12) to learn the difference between a poussin and a capon and which cooks faster. You'll also discover handy how-to basics sifted through the pages, such as "how to tell when a chicken is done" and Time Savers, such as fixing two dinners at once (page 112).

Along the way, we've tucked in a wealth of answers to common food questions, like how to stretch your dollars in the supermarket. Look in the Food Facts box (page 130) to find out which is the least expensive cut of chicken, pound for pound. For your health's sake, check out the latest safety steps for choosing, using, cleaning chopping boards, according to the United States Department of Agriculture (page 65). You'll even find simple explanations for why some techniques work the way they do, like the osmosis principle behind brining that yields the juiciest chicken breast ever, and other little-known facts, like what "chicken of the woods" is (the answer's on page 99).

Enjoy discovering all the recipes and high-speed hints we've loaded into *Terrific Chicken*, knowing that you can look forward to even more great cooking ideas in the other books in our collection. Each book is designed to focus on a specific type of food and provides just what you want in today's cookbooks—quick-cooking recipes, beautiful photographs, useful techniques, and handy tips—and is guaranteed to become a "fast kitchen friend." We've created each book in this quick cooking collection to be not only fun to browse through, but also so jam-packed that you'll find yourself referring to, and using, each one time and again. With so many great homemade (and better tasting!) meals in less time than ever, you can transform your usual "rush hour" into a "relaxing hour."

Here's to good cooking—with *Terrific Chicken!*

Tortilla-crusted Chicken Paillard, page 138

Fresh Ideas with Chicken

Here it is, all in one book—many new terrific ways, plus those tried-and-true ways too, for cooking *Terrific Chicken*, faster and easier than ever before. Discover how our new collection can save you time and help you put excitement into mealtimes like you never thought possible. It all begins right inside this chapter. We've collected six of our favorite ways to make the most of chicken, giving you tips, techniques, and the principles behind each new method. Plus, we've added ways to help you save time by using shortcuts at every step. Once you learn the latest of what the pros—and other cooks just like you—are doing with chicken, you're well on your way to mixing up your own terrific chicken creations.

BLAST-OFF ROAST CHICKEN

Roast the juiciest chicken every time by following three simple quick cooking techniques: butterfly it…rub it… blast it. Start by picking the right bird—one that carries the "roaster" label. These birds are a little older and larger (weighing in at least 5 pounds) and have developed more muscle tissue than broilers or fryers. Each roaster brings a thicker layer of fat into the oven, which melts away, self-basting the bird as it cooks.

BUTTERFLYING THE BIRD (the chefs call it *spatch-cocking*)—This is just a fancy word that means to simply remove the breastbone and then flatten the bird out with your hands. This technique cuts roasting time in half!

RUB IT IN—The next step: rubbing in the spices. Start with a dry rub (that's a mixture of herbs and spices) and work it into a softened butter to make a thick flavor-paste. Gently smear the paste directly onto the bird underneath the skin with your hands, taking care not to tear the skin. For an easy herb-flavored paste, chop up fresh herbs, like fresh rosemary, sage, and thyme and blend them into the butter. For a fast seasoned paste, seek out the many spice blends in your supermarket, such as lemon-pepper, Jamaican jerk, Indian curry, Szechuan, Louisiana-Cajun, herbes de Provence, and Thai. Add about a teaspoon to a stick of softened butter to make ½ cup of paste, then taste it. Add a little more seasoning, if you like.

BLAST IT! Put the roaster in a very hot 475°F oven for 15 to 20 minutes, and then turn it down to 375°F for the rest of the roasting. This high heat kills off any bacteria on the chicken skin and sets off a complex "browning" reaction between the sugars and proteins. This turns the bird that golden brown color, gives it a crusty skin, and adds that delicious caramelized flavor. By blasting the butterflied bird with this burst of high heat, you'll be able to take it out of the oven in just about 40 minutes—or less!

Grilled Chicken Satays, page 107

Skillet Italiano, page 83

Asian Coleslaw, page 51

MAGIC FROM THE SALTY SEAS

Salting—the simplest technique of flavoring and preserving meats—has been around for centuries. But it's just lately become "fashionable" with chefs and good home cooks when working with chicken. Rub a whole chicken or chicken pieces with sea salt or kosher salt: ½ to ¾ teaspoon kosher salt per pound of chicken (a heaping tablespoon for a 7-pound roaster). Rub salt all over the bird, inside and out, then cover with plastic wrap and refrigerate it up to 2 hours. As the bird rests in the refrigerator, the salt works to pull moisture from the chicken. Simultaneously, salt renders the meat more tender by actually changing the proteins of the chicken cells so they can accept more moisture than before. At the end of the process, the chicken reabsorbs the moisture that was lost, along with the salt, which enhances that real chicken flavor. This results in plumping up the bird, making it juicier than ever.

Cooking Basics

7 HIGH-SPEED SUPPERS FROM CHICKEN BREASTS

Flatten it, season it, coat it, sauté it. Chicken breast fillets make quick and easy meals. Buy 4 or 5 ounces of boneless, skinless chicken breast halves per serving. Choose the pre pounded fillets or buy the thicker chicken breast halves and pound them thin with a meat mallet at home. The pounding goes faster if you put the chicken between plastic wrap first to prevent sticking. Season the thin fillets and coat them with flour or crumbs, choosing from the ideas here. Then simply sauté chicken in 1 tablespoon each of butter and oil for 1 to 2 minutes per side, or until light brown and juices run clear. Supper's ready to serve in a matter of minutes!

QUICK SOUTHWESTERN WAY Coat chicken with flour seasoned with chili powder. Sauté and serve with barbecue sauce.

SPEEDY CAJUN WAY Pat chicken with a mix of black pepper, ground red pepper, and Cajun seasonings. Sauté and garnish with a few minced hot chilies.

FAST ITALIAN WAY Coat chicken with Italian-seasoned dry bread crumbs and sauté. Splash with Marsala wine the last minute.

THE HAWAIIAN WAY Splash the skillet with pineapple juice and sprinkle with chopped macadamia nuts.

QUICK JAMAICAN WAY Coat chicken with flour spiked with jerk seasonings and sauté. Add a splash of strong coffee to the skillet the last minute.

FABULOUS FRENCH WAY Whisk 2 eggs with 1 tablespoon of water. Dip chicken into egg mixture and coat with ground almonds, then sauté. Add a splash of white wine to the skillet during the last minute.

THE CALIFORNIA WAY Coat chicken with seasoned flour, then sauté. Splash in the juice of a lemon and an orange during the last minute of cooking. Sprinkle with toasted walnuts.

JUICE UP CHICKEN BY BRINING

Take a tip from the pros: Brining works wonders on chicken! It's a method best used on pieces, rather than the whole bird. Whisk up a basic brine: ¼ cup Kosher salt, ¼ cup sugar, and 4 cups of water. Add a touch of extra flavor with a garlic clove plus a sprig of fresh rosemary or thyme. Pour the brine over the chicken, and let "brine" for 15 minutes at room temperature, or up to 2 hours in the refrigerator. As the chicken soaks, the brine goes to work—tenderizing, flavoring, and keeping meat moist.

Cooking Basics

GREAT & FAST PICK-ME-UPS FROM THE CHICKEN CASE

Look carefully…you'll find chicken arriving in markets in new and interesting ways these days. Naturally the standbys are there, such as boneless thighs, chicken quarters, and family paks (we've not listed them, as they're already familiar favorites). Here, a few new cuts…old-favorites in new ways…others that come table-ready:

POUSSIN Tiny, tender, and elegant chickens, usually under 1 pound (perfect to serve one to each guest). Roast them under a red currant or orange marmalade glaze—and they're ready to serve in less than 40 minutes.

CAPON Wonderful flavor and very tender meat…terrific roasted or poached. A capon is a 7- to 9-pound male bird with a high proportion of light meat to dark. You might have to special-order it.

ROTISSERIE CHICKEN A fast pick-me-up from your neighborhood take-out food shop or market. Keep it at room temperature if you're eating within an hour, or else refrigerate. To reheat, just pop into the microwave for a minute.

CHICKEN & VEGGIE KABOBS Often found in specialty meat markets or gourmet stores, already assembled and ready for the grille. Many come in their own marinades, such as Hawaiian Sweet & Sour, Thai, Korean Sesame, Honey Jalapeño, and Texas Barbecue.

CARVED & READY-TO- EAT! Thanks to new manufacturing innovations, cooked chicken comes carved and ready to microwave (or not) and eat. Perfect for tossing into salads, adding to soups, stacking in sandwiches, or just eating as is, straight from its sealed packet. These often come mesquite-roasted or smoked and spiced.

GROUND CHICKEN A great alternative to ground beef, with only about half the fat. Use in recipes where the meat is cooked well done, such as tacos, meatloaf, or chili. Look for shaped patties too, often seasoned Cajun-style and perfect for the grill.

FROM A CAN Don't forget one of the most convenient forms of chicken—ready to toss into a salad in an instant.

CHICKEN SAUSAGE A good way to buy sausage, with a lot of flavor and much less fat. Look for Italian-pesto sausages or New Orleans–spiced ones called andouille.

Mediterranean Chicken Breasts, page 34

CUT COOKING TIME WITH A MALLET!

Take a tip from cooks in France: Pound a boneless, skinless chicken breast until it's very thin, about ¼ inch thick. The French call it a *paillard* (thin piece), also an *escalope*. All you need is a flat meat pounder or heavy pot (see page 83 for all the details). As you pound away, take care to flatten it evenly all over. Then cook the paillard in a hot skillet or on a hot, slightly oiled grill—in 2 minutes flat. Now that's fast! Have fun with the finishing touches. Sprinkle on a few hot chili flakes, a little roasted minced garlic, some finely chopped fresh tomato and slivered basil, a splash of fresh lemon juice, a drizzle of balsamic vinegar, or a squirt of herb-flavored oil.

THERE'S A CHICKEN UNDER THAT BRICK!

The Italians call this chicken *Pollo al Matone* (translated from Italian, that's "chicken under a brick"). This method has truly stood the test of centuries of cooking chicken. And it works whether you're sautéing chicken in a skillet, baking it in an oven, or grilling it on a grill, First, wrap the brick in foil. If you don't have a brick handy, use a heavy iron skillet, as it works just as well, though it doesn't make quite the same "conversation piece" with guests. Place the brick on the chicken and start roasting, sautéing, or grilling. As the chicken cooks, the brick compacts and weighs down the meat so it cooks more evenly, allowing the outside of the chicken to brown and crisp without drying out. Plus, when you use this brick method on the grill, it presses the chicken against the grill grate, leaving great grill marks.

SOAKING IN THE FLAVOR

Go ahead…marinate any cut of chicken you wish. It's simply another great, quick way to get delicious, flavor-bursting chicken! Put simply, a marinade is a highly flavored, concentrated, seasoned liquid that tenderizes the exterior of the chicken and helps the meat accept the flavor of the marinade. Marinades usually contain an acid (such as buttermilk, vinegar, wine, and citrus or fruit juices) plus an oil to slow down the marinating action and to baste the chicken while it's cooking. Experiment with marinades as much as you like—especially with boneless, skinless chicken breasts. Just be sure to watch the clock, because it's easy to overmarinate. Unless a recipe indicates otherwise, as a general rule, chicken breasts should marinate at room temperature for only about 15 minutes, as they can become mushy and stringy if they marinate for even 30 minutes. Marinate a whole bird in the refrigerator for 6 to 24 hours.

Try our Thai soy (page 104), our lemon–Dijon (page 114), and our white wine–herb marinade (page 123). If you're in a hurry, just pick up a marinade from the sauce section in your supermarket. You might want to try Sweet & Sour Mesquite…Bombay Mango…Jamaican Jerk.

Browse through *Terrific Chicken* and pick out a few recipes, then head to the kitchen and start cooking. Here are some of our quick favorites you might want to try:

Savory Lemon Chicken Skillet (page 19)

California Lime Chicken (page 20)

Stir-fry Salad (page 47)

Chicken & Pepper Heroes (page 66)

Ranch Pizza Pie (page 75)

Pennsylvania Dutch Chicken Bake (page 89)

Teriyaki Rice Bowl, (page 90)

Easy Barbecue Kabobs (page 102)

Surf 'n' Turf Grill (page 109)

Cherry-glazed Chicken (page 124)

Tortilla-crusted Chicken Paillard (page 138)

Cherry-glazed Chicken, page 124

Pennsylvania Dutch Chicken Bake, page 89

Ranch Pizza Pie, page 75

Quick Chicken Stir-fry, page 22

Sizzling Skillets

Looking for "something simple, sizzling, and simply delicious" for supper? Reach for a skillet, some chicken, and a few ingredients that you probably have on-hand. Choose your favorite recipe from our collection here. For instance, try chicken breasts straight from the skillet with a twist of lemon, a spice of mustard, or slivers of fresh herbs. Sauce up chicken with cranberries, green grapes, fresh oranges, apples, or a made-in-minutes Dijon sauce. Or team up a chicken with wild rice or turn it Oriental with a teriyaki sauce. However you slice it, fry it, spice it, bread it, toss it, or simmer it, sizzling chicken from the skillet is a great supper—quick and good!

SuperQuick

CHICKEN WITH OLD-STYLE DIJON MUSTARD SAUCE

Prep **5 MINUTES**   *Cook* **25 MINUTES**

Grab a skillet, some chicken and this recipe the next time you're cooking for company on the spur of the moment. Add a fresh salad and a crusty loaf of bread, and dinner's ready in minutes.

4	boneless, skinless chicken breast halves (about 1¼ pounds)
3	tablespoons whole-grain Dijon mustard
2	tablespoons extra-virgin olive oil
2	shallots, finely chopped
½	cup dry white wine or water
½	cup reduced-sodium chicken broth
2	tablespoons heavy cream
	Salt and ground black pepper
	Cooked angel hair pasta (optional)

LET'S BEGIN Brush the chicken with the mustard. Heat the oil in a large skillet over medium-high heat. Pan-fry the chicken, turning once, for 6 minutes, or until golden brown. Stir in the shallots, wine, and broth and bring to a boil.

SIMMER SLOW Cover, reduce the heat, and simmer for 10 minutes, or until the chicken juices run clear. Transfer the chicken to a platter and keep warm.

SAUCE & SERVE Add the cream to the pan juices and simmer, whisking constantly, until the sauce reduces slightly. Season with salt and pepper and spoon over the chicken. Serve with pasta, if you like.

Makes 4 servings

Per serving: 290 calories, 34g protein, 4g carbohydrates, 13g fat, 3g saturated fat, 93mg cholesterol, 325mg sodium

Cooking Basics

SECRETS TO SPEEDY SAUTÉS

START WITH HOT!
When sautéing, heat the empty skillet until hot. Then add the oil, heat a minute, and slide in the food. This quick-starts the cooking, ensuring chicken browns fast and evenly.

PAN-FRYING PRETTY
When you sauté chicken breasts, your finished dish will look its best if you use the heaviest skillet you own, check that the oil is clear and fresh, and fry the prettiest, plumpest part first. Make sure to turn the food only once during cooking, as the first side to hit the skillet always fries up the most attractively.

JUMPING FOOD
In French, the word *sauté* is derived from the verb "to jump." During the perfect sauté, the food actually does "jump" in the skillet. For the best results, cut the food into small strips or pieces, shake the pan, and toss the food constantly as you cook.

SAVORY LEMON CHICKEN SKILLET

Prep **5 MINUTES**   *Cook* **15 MINUTES**

4	boneless, skinless chicken breast halves (about 1¼ pounds)

Salt and ground black pepper

¼	cup all-purpose flour
1	tablespoon vegetable oil
1	cup chicken broth
1⅓	cups french-fried onions
1	tablespoon lemon juice
4	thin lemon slices

The crunch of onion rings and the fragrant burst of lemon bring surprise flavors to this easy weeknight meal. Watch the dish make its own sauce as it simmers.

LET'S BEGIN Sprinkle the chicken with salt and pepper. Coat with the flour, shaking off the excess.

SAUTÉ IT QUICK Heat the oil in a large nonstick skillet over medium-high heat. Cook the chicken, turning once, for 6 minutes, or until golden brown.

SIMMER & SERVE Stir in the broth, ⅔ cup of the fried onions, and the lemon juice and slices. Bring to a boil, then reduce the heat. Cover and simmer, stirring occasionally, for 5 to 10 minutes, or until the chicken juices run clear and the sauce thickens slightly. Sprinkle the remaining fried onions on top of the chicken just before serving.

Makes 4 servings

Per serving: 350 calories, 35g protein, 16g carbohydrates, 15g fat, 4g saturated fat, 82mg cholesterol, 520mg sodium

CALIFORNIA LIME CHICKEN

Prep **10 MINUTES**   *Cook* **30 MINUTES**

Out in California, where fruit groves are all around, cooking with citrus is common. Try this simple sizzle, sparkled up with fresh lime, tarragon, and a splash of hot pepper sauce.

¼	cup butter or margarine
4	chicken breast halves (about 2 pounds)
1	tablespoon fresh tarragon or ½ teaspoon dried
1	teaspoon salt
2	tablespoons lime juice
2	tablespoons water
½	teaspoon hot pepper sauce

Hot cooked rice (optional)

LET'S BEGIN Melt the butter in a large skillet over medium heat. Place the chicken in the skillet, skin side down, and season with half of the tarragon and ½ teaspoon of the salt. Cook for 10 minutes, or until the chicken is brown. Turn the chicken and sprinkle with the remaining tarragon and salt. Cook 10 minutes longer, or until the second side is brown.

SIMMER LOW Combine the lime juice, water, and hot pepper sauce in a small bowl and pour over the chicken. Reduce the heat. Cover and simmer for 10 minutes, or until the chicken juices run clear.

SERVE IT UP Serve the chicken over hot cooked rice, if you like.

> *Makes 4 servings*
> *Per serving: 360 calories, 30g protein, 1g carbohydrates, 26g fat, 11g saturated fat, 126mg cholesterol, 800mg sodium*

Food Facts

CHICKEN, A NUTRITION POWERHOUSE

PACKED WITH PROTEIN
There's plenty of high-quality protein (and iron too!) in chicken. A 3½-ounce serving of cooked chicken breast (without the skin) provides over 60 percent of the Daily Value for protein. And surprisingly, it weighs in at only 165 calories! Plus it supplies over 30 percent of the Daily Value for vitamin B_6, which helps the body build proteins and make other red blood cells.

SKIN THAT BIRD!
Removing the skin from the chicken not only lowers the calories but also cuts the total fat and saturated fat in half.

GO FOR LIGHT MEAT
Roasted, skinless light chicken meat from the breast has only 3 grams of total fat and 1 gram of saturated fat in a 3-ounce serving. In comparison, roasted, skinless dark meat chicken from the leg or thigh has more than three times the total fat (10 grams) and three times the saturated fat (3 grams). Cholesterol, however, in both light and dark meat is similar.

APPLE-CRANBERRY CHICKEN MARSALA

Prep **10 MINUTES**   *Cook* **10 MINUTES**

4	boneless, skinless chicken breast halves (about 1¼ pounds)

Salt and ground black pepper

2	tablespoons butter or margarine
⅓	cup Marsala wine or cranberry juice
2	tablespoons apple jelly
2	Granny Smith apples, peeled, cored, and cut into ¼-inch-thick slices
½	cup dried cranberries

Dried cranberries add both sweet and tart flavors to this autumn combination of thinly sliced apples and quickly pan-fried golden brown chicken. Supper's ready fast!

LET'S BEGIN Season the chicken with salt and pepper. Melt the butter in a large skillet over medium-high heat.

QUICK COOK Add the chicken and cook, turning once, for 6 minutes, or until golden brown and the juices run clear. Transfer the chicken to a platter and keep warm.

SAUCE IT Add the wine, jelly, and apples to the skillet. Bring to a boil, turning the apples and scraping up the brown bits in the bottom of the pan. Add the cranberries and cook 1 minute longer, or until the sauce thickens slightly. Spoon the apple-cranberry sauce over the chicken.

Makes 4 servings

Per serving: 305 calories, 27g protein, 25g carbohydrates, 9g fat, 4g saturated fat, 89mg cholesterol, 130mg sodium

CHICKEN & RICE L'ORANGE

Prep **10 MINUTES**   *Cook* **16 MINUTES**

1	cup long-grain white rice
1	cup orange juice
1	cup water
1	teaspoon salt
3	tablespoons butter or margarine
¼	cup sliced almonds
4	boneless, skinless chicken breast halves (about 1¼ pounds)
¼	cup sweet orange marmalade
¼	cup sliced scallion

With this fast yet elegant dish, add snow peas. Dinner is done!

LET'S BEGIN Bring the first 4 ingredients to a boil in a medium saucepan, stirring once or twice. Reduce the heat. Cover and simmer for 15 minutes, or until the liquid is absorbed. Meanwhile, melt 1 tablespoon of butter in a large skillet over medium-high heat. Add the almonds and cook, stirring, for 2 minutes, or until golden. Transfer to a dish.

SIMMER & GLAZE Melt the remaining butter in the same skillet. Cook the chicken, turning once, for 12 minutes, or until juices run clear. Stir in the marmalade until melted.

SERVE Mound the rice onto a platter and top with the chicken. Sprinkle with the almonds and scallion.

> *Makes 4 servings*
>
> Per serving: 524 calories, 33g protein, 59g carbohydrates, 17g fat, 7g saturated fat, 99mg cholesterol, 774mg sodium

QUICK CHICKEN STIR-FRY

Prep **10 MINUTES**   *Cook* **7 MINUTES**

1	cup minute rice
1	tablespoon oil
1	pound boneless, skinless chicken breast halves, cut into strips
3	cups sliced vegetables, such as bell peppers, carrots, mushrooms, and broccoli florets
¼	cup stir-fry sauce

Whip up this stir-fry even faster by using frozen vegetables.

LET'S BEGIN Cook the rice according to package directions and keep warm. Meanwhile, heat the oil in a large skillet over medium-high heat for 1 minute.

STIR-FRY Add the chicken. Stir-fry for 5 minutes, or until brown. Stir in the vegetables and cook 5 minutes longer.

TOSS & SERVE Pour in the sauce, cover, and cook for 2 minutes, or until hot. Serve over the rice.

> *Makes 3 servings*
>
> Per serving: 340 calories, 34g protein, 49g carbohydrates, 7g fat, 2g saturated fat, 40mg cholesterol, 1,030mg sodium

Chicken & Rice l'Orange

SuperQuick
CHICKEN VÉRONIQUE
Prep **10 MINUTES**   *Cook* **15 MINUTES**

2   tablespoons vegetable oil

4   boneless, skinless chicken breast halves (1¼ pounds)

2   tablespoons sugar

1   cup dry white wine

1   cup chicken stock or broth

1   tablespoon cornstarch

1½   cups seedless California grapes

Though the original recipe may not have come from France, this dish has an elegant wine sauce the French are famous for—yet it cooks in a flash. Serve with buttered noodles and minted baby peas.

LET'S BEGIN   Heat the oil in a large pan over medium-high heat. Add the chicken and sauté, turning once, for 6 minutes, or until golden brown. Remove the chicken from the pan and pour off the excess oil.

MAKE IT SAUCY   Add the sugar and half of the wine, stirring to dissolve the sugar. Add the remaining wine and simmer until the mixture is reduced by half.

SIMMER & SERVE   Mix the stock and cornstarch in a small bowl. Whisk into the wine mixture and simmer for 2 minutes. Return the chicken to the sauce. Add the grapes and simmer for 2 minutes longer, or until the juices run clear.

Makes 4 servings

Per serving: 340 calories, 34g protein, 19g carbohydrates, 9g fat, 1g saturated fat, 82mg cholesterol, 290mg sodium

---

Food Facts

ALL ABOARD! CHICKEN'S ON THE MENU IN THE DINING CAR

Passengers on board the railways in their hey day, from the 1890s to the 1950s, traveled luxuriously and dined well. The trains were elegant hotels on wheels—from the early Victorian parlor cars to the sleek art deco diners of the 1930s.

The menu featured local fresh foods the train picked up on its stops through the countryside. A seven-course dinner cost only a dollar, and what great eating!

Chicken was often on the menu, for it was fast, simple to cook in the small galley, and versatile enough to offer great variety.

Steaming bowls of Chicken Gumbo were a specialty on the Southern Pacific railway as it sped through the Deep South. The chefs on the Great Northern baked chicken pies, and those on the Southern Pacific fried up crispy chicken with rich cream gravy.

SuperQuick

CONCORD SIZZLE

Prep **10 MINUTES** *Cook* **20 MINUTES**

Concord grape juice teams up with chicken and tarragon in a winning skillet sauté. Dinner's ready in just half an hour!

¼ cup all-purpose flour

Salt and ground black pepper

4 boneless, skinless chicken breast halves (about 1¼ pounds)

3 tablespoons butter or margarine

½ cup 100% Concord grape juice

½ cup chicken broth

½ teaspoon dried tarragon

¼ cup half-and-half

1 to 2 teaspoons lemon juice

Lemon slices

LET'S BEGIN Mix together the flour, salt, and pepper on a piece of waxed paper. Coat the chicken breasts with the seasoned flour, shaking off the excess.

SAUTÉ IT QUICK Melt the butter in a large nonstick skillet over medium-high heat. Cook the chicken, turning once, for 15 minutes, or until golden brown and the juices run clear. Transfer to a platter and keep warm.

SAUCE & SERVE Add the grape juice and broth to the skillet and stir to loosen the brown bits in the bottom of the skillet. Whisk in the tarragon and half-and-half and cook for 3 minutes, or until it thickens slightly. Season with salt and pepper and stir in the lemon juice. Spoon the sauce over the chicken and garnish with the lemon slices.

Makes 4 servings

Per serving: 310 calories, 35g protein, 12g carbohydrates, 13g fat, 7g saturated fat, 112mg cholesterol, 360mg sodium

---

Time Savers

5 FAST HINTS FOR FASTER COOKING

BUY BONELESS
Put boneless chicken (thighs and breasts) into the braising pot. Cuts cooking time in half!

SKIP BROWNING
If you're really in a hurry, skip browning the chicken or other meat in your braising pot. You'll find that you'll save on cooking time and avoid splattering up the kitchen with oil, too.

MAKE A SPEEDY CUT
Cook boneless, skinless chicken breast halves even faster by cutting each fillet horizontally into two thin equal pieces with a boning knife. They'll cook in about 5 minutes—not the normal time of 12 to 15 minutes.

ADD OIL THIS WAY
When you're frying or sautéing chicken and you need more oil, drizzle it down the side of the skillet. By the time it reaches the food, it'll be hot. The temperature in the skillet stays the same, and the food keeps cooking.

KEEP IT MOVING
To brown meat fast, place it first in the hot center of the skillet then move to the cooler side to finish cooking.

LINGUINE PRIMAVERA PARMESAN

Prep **10 MINUTES**   *Cook* **7 MINUTES**

4	ounces fresh linguine
2	tablespoons olive oil
2	cups cut-up mixed fresh vegetables, such as broccoli florets, carrots, bell peppers, and zucchini
1	package (6 ounces) grilled chicken breast strips
⅓	cup grated Parmesan cheese

By cutting the vegetables small, this dish of fresh linguine, pregrilled chicken, and lovely fresh veggies is even faster to fix!

LET'S BEGIN Half-fill a large saucepan with salted water and bring to a boil. Add the linguine and cook for 2 minutes, then drain and keep hot.

COOK & TOSS Meanwhile, heat the oil in a large non-stick skillet over medium-high heat. Sauté the vegetables for 5 minutes, or until crisp-tender. Add the chicken and pasta. Cook and toss the mixture 2 minutes longer, or until heated through. Add the Parmesan and toss well.

> *Makes 2 servings*
>
> *Per serving: 380 calories, 25g protein, 34g carbohydrates, 16g fat, 5g saturated fat, 50mg cholesterol, 730mg sodium*

LEMON-OLIVE CHICKEN & WILD RICE

Prep **10 MINUTES**   *Cook* **30 MINUTES**

2	tablespoons olive oil
1	broiler-fryer, cut up or 3 pounds chicken pieces
2	tablespoons lemon juice
1	package long-grain and wild rice mix
1	can (8 ounces) pitted ripe medium olives, drained
1	large tomato, chopped
2½	cups reduced-sodium chicken broth

Dine Mediterranean style by stirring up this simple skillet pilaf.

SAUTÉ IT QUICK Heat the oil in a large nonstick skillet over medium-high heat. Cook the chicken, turning once, for 6 minutes, or until golden brown.

FIX IT FAST Add the remaining ingredients to the skillet.

SIMMER & SERVE Bring to a boil, then reduce the heat. Cover and simmer for 20 minutes, or until all of the liquid is absorbed.

> *Makes 4 servings*
>
> *Per serving: 590 calories, 33g protein, 38g carbohydrates, 35g fat, 8g saturated fat, 106mg cholesterol, 1,660mg sodium*

Linguine Primavera Parmesan

SPANISH HOLIDAY

Prep **10 MINUTES**   *Cook* **20 MINUTES**

3   large red bell peppers
(2 halved, 1 sliced into
thin strips)

2   teaspoons white wine
vinegar

½   teaspoons hot pepper
sauce

Salt

3   tablespoons olive oil

4   chicken breast halves
(about 2 pounds)

Ground black pepper
(optional)

In Spain, peppers pop up in many of the dishes. Roast the peppers and whirl them into a sauce early in the day. Or just use preroasted peppers instead. Later, sizzle up supper in 20 minutes flat.

LET'S BEGIN Preheat the broiler. Broil the 4 pepper halves about 5 inches from the heat for 5 minutes on each side, or until lightly charred. Transfer to a brown paper bag, close tightly, steam for 10 minutes, and slip off the skins.

PROCESS SMOOTH Purée the roasted peppers, vinegar, hot pepper sauce, and ¼ teaspoon salt in a food processor or blender. Gradually add 1 tablespoon of the oil and process until smooth (you will have about ½ cup sauce). Set aside.

SAUTÉ IT QUICK Heat the remaining oil in a heavy skillet over high heat. Season the chicken with salt and pepper, if you like, and sauté for 8 minutes on each side, or until the juices run clear. Add sliced peppers and cook 2 minutes longer, or until soft. Serve with the pepper sauce.

Makes 4 servings

Per serving: 372 calories, 31g protein, 8g carbohydrates, 24g fat, 5g saturated fat, 93mg cholesterol, 243mg sodium

Cooking Basics

LOOK FOR THE "FRESH" LABEL

The best way to be sure you're buying the better-tasting bird is to look for the "fresh" label when choosing a package of chicken. According to the United States Department of Agriculture (USDA), birds displaying the "fresh" tag have been stored at temperatures between 26°F and 32°F on their way to the poultry case. (You might see a few ice crystals, but don't worry…the bird's still fresh!) When a chicken has been stored at temperatures below 0°F, the USDA requires the bird to wear a "frozen" label.

QUICK HONEY FRIED CHICKEN

Prep **5 MINUTES**   *Cook* **25 MINUTES**

Honey makes a big difference in this dish. It helps the coating adhere to the chicken during frying. Serve as they do in the South with collard greens and sweet-potato fries.

1	chicken (about 3 pounds), cut up or chicken pieces
¾	cup honey
¾	to 1 cup buttermilk baking mix
2	teaspoons dry mustard
½	teaspoon paprika
	Salt and ground black pepper
	Vegetable oil for frying

LET'S BEGIN Coat the chicken with the honey. Combine the buttermilk baking mix, mustard, and paprika and season with salt and pepper.

LET IT BROWN Heat ½ inch oil until hot (375°F) but not smoking in a large deep skillet over medium heat. Lower the chicken into the oil and cook, turning with tongs as needed, for 10 minutes, or until light golden brown on all sides.

SIMMER & SERVE Reduce the heat to low but do not cover! Cook the chicken for 15 minutes, or until the juices run clear. Using tongs, transfer chicken to cooling racks to drain.

Makes 4 servings

Per serving: 640 calories, 29g protein, 67g carbohydrates, 30g fat, 7g saturated fat, 106mg cholesterol, 450mg sodium

Cook to Cook

WHAT'S YOUR SECRET TO PERFECT SOUTHERN FRIED CHICKEN THAT'S COOKED ON THE INSIDE, BUT NOT BURNT?

"I cook my chicken *in the cast-iron skillet my grandmother passed down to me.* It's so heavy that it holds in the heat and browns the chicken perfectly every time.

After breading chicken, I always **chill it before frying.** Refrigerate it on a small rack, without covering, for about an hour to firm up the coating.

If the oil has not reached the smoking stage during cooking, you can reuse it. First, let the oil cool, then strain it though a cheesecloth. Store it in a closed jar in the refrigerator. Use it later for cooking the same type of foods. Tip: Never cook chicken in oil that fish has been fried in.

When the chicken's done, **let it drain on a rack**— never on paper towels. This way, the chicken stays crisp and doesn't turn soggy."

SuperQuick

BREAST OF CHICKEN BALSAMIC

Prep **5 MINUTES**   *Cook* **25 MINUTES**

4	boneless, skinless chicken breast halves (about 1¼ pounds)
2	teaspoons extra-virgin olive oil
8	ounces white mushrooms, quartered
2	garlic cloves, minced
½	cup reduced-sodium chicken broth
2½	tablespoons balsamic vinegar
¼	teaspoon dried thyme, crushed
⅛	teaspoon ground black pepper
Chopped fresh parsley	

Balsamic vinegar and sautéed mushrooms make this quickly made chicken sauté burst with flavor. Your guests will never suspect that it's low in fat as well.

LET'S BEGIN Spray a large nonstick skillet with cooking spray and set over medium heat. Cook the chicken, turning once, for 6 minutes, or until golden brown. Transfer to a plate and keep warm.

SAUTÉ IT QUICK Add the oil to the skillet. Sauté the mushrooms and garlic for 3 minutes, or until the garlic is fragrant. Return the chicken to the pan and add the broth, vinegar, thyme, and pepper. Reduce the heat and simmer, covered, for 15 minutes, or until the chicken juices run clear.

TOP & SERVE Transfer the chicken to a platter and top with the mushrooms and pan sauce. Sprinkle with parsley.

Makes 4 servings

Per serving: 138 calories, 20g protein, 6g carbohydrates, 4g fat, 1g saturated fat, 43mg cholesterol, 248mg sodium

---

Food Facts

DRIZZLING ON THE BALSAMIC, WITHOUT GOING BROKE!

COMMERCIAL BALSAMIC Most commercial balsamics are made from red wine vinegar, with a little caramel added. Sometimes, boiled-down grape musk is used to increase the flavor. While these don't have the complexities (or the high price!) of true balsamic vinegar, they are great for cooking, salads, and marinades.

To enhance any type of commercial balsamic, boil 1 cup of the vinegar in a small uncovered saucepan until it thickens and forms a syrup. Add a spoonful of brown sugar, stirring until it melts, to smooth out the flavor. This syrup is great when drizzled over fresh fruit, such as blackberries, strawberries, raspberries, and fresh peaches.

THE REAL BALSAMIC VINEGAR True balsamic vinegar (the real stuff) is very expensive but worth the cost—especially when used drop by drop over grilled meats or tossed with berries. Real balsamic vinegar (aged 50 to 100 years) is made from concentrated white Trebbiano grape juice. No cooking, please, for heat destroys its flavor.

SuperQuick
PICK OF THE GARDEN
Prep **10 MINUTES**   *Cook* **16 MINUTES**

1   tablespoon olive oil

4   boneless, skinless
     chicken breast halves
     (about 1¼ pounds)

1   tablespoon chopped
     fresh oregano or
     1 teaspoon dried or
     ½ teaspoon dried
     rosemary, crushed

Salt and ground black pepper
(optional)

1   can (14½ ounces)
     diced tomatoes with
     garlic and onion

1   green bell pepper, cut
     into thin strips

1   large carrot, cut into
     matchsticks

1   medium zucchini, cut
     into matchsticks

Small pitted ripe olives
(optional)

Fresh oregano sprigs
(optional)

Hot cooked rice (optional)

Thinly cut veggies and chopped herbs make this quickly cooked chicken fresh and zesty. For a change of pace, substitute red or yellow peppers for the green.

LET'S BEGIN Heat the oil in a large nonstick skillet over medium-high heat. Cook the chicken, turning once, for 6 minutes, or until golden brown. Sprinkle with the oregano and season with salt and pepper, if you like.

QUICK COOK Add all of the remaining ingredients except the olives, oregano sprigs, and rice and bring to a boil. Reduce the heat. Cover and simmer for 3 minutes. Uncover, and cook over medium-high heat for 5 minutes, or until the chicken juices run clear. Transfer to a platter.

SAUCE & SERVE Garnish with olives and oregano sprigs and serve with rice, if desired.

Makes 4 servings
Per serving: 250 calories, 35g protein, 14g carbohydrates, 5g fat, 1g saturated fat, 82mg cholesterol, 630mg sodium

SuperQuick
CHICKEN-VEGETABLE TERIYAKI

Prep **5 MINUTES**   Cook **20 MINUTES**

This super-fast pan-fry uses salty-sweet teriyaki sauce, crisp sugar snaps, and boneless chicken. Serve it with steamed rice, and your guests will think they've just visited the Orient.

1	tablespoon vegetable oil
4	boneless, skinless chicken breast halves (about 1¼ pounds), cut into strips
1	bag (16 ounces) frozen stir-fry vegetables with sugar snaps
⅔	cup teriyaki chicken sauté sauce with ginger and sesame
⅓	cup slivered almonds, toasted
	Hot cooked rice (optional)

LET'S BEGIN Heat the oil in a large nonstick skillet over medium-high heat. Add the chicken and pan-fry, turning once, for 6 minutes or until golden brown. Transfer to a plate and keep warm.

SAUTÉ IT QUICK Add the vegetables to the skillet and sauté for about 10 minutes, or until crisp-tender.

SAUCE & SERVE Return the chicken to the skillet and pour in the teriyaki sauce, tossing to coat. Cook 2 minutes longer, or until heated through. Sprinkle with the almonds. Serve over rice, if desired.

Makes 4 servings

Per serving: 350 calories, 42g protein, 22g carbohydrates, 11g fat, 1g saturated fat, 82mg cholesterol, 2,060mg sodium

---

On the Menu

Quickly turn the whole meal Oriental. Pick up egg rolls and fresh pineapple spears on your way home.

Bite-size Egg Rolls

Chicken-Vegetable Teriyaki

Rice with Sautéed Scallions

Fresh Pineapple with Vanilla Ice Cream

Pot of Jasmine Tea

SuperQuick
MEDITERRANEAN CHICKEN BREASTS

Prep **10 MINUTES**   *Cook* **15 MINUTES**

½   cup grated Pecorino Romano cheese

¼   cup plain dry bread crumbs

1   teaspoon dried basil

¼   teaspoon paprika

¼   teaspoon salt

¼   teaspoon black pepper

3   tablespoons olive oil

6   large boneless, skinless chicken breast halves (about 2 pounds)

For crispy chicken, this Mediterranean-style is one of the quickest around. Toss some pasta and add a baby spinach salad. You're set!

LET'S BEGIN Mix together the first 6 ingredients on a piece of waxed paper. Put the oil in a shallow dish.

DIP & COAT Dip the chicken in the oil, then coat evenly with the cheese mixture.

SAUTÉ & SERVE Spray a skillet with cooking spray and set over medium heat. Add the chicken and cook, turning once, for 15 minutes, or until golden and the juices run clear.

> *Makes 6 servings*
>
> *Per serving: 270 calories, 38g protein, 19g carbohydrates, 11g fat, 3g saturated fat, 95mg cholesterol, 314mg sodium*

SuperQuick
SWEET & SPICY STIR-FRY

Prep **10 MINUTES**   *Cook* **20 MINUTES**

⅓   cup pineapple juice

2   teaspoons cornstarch

⅓   cup soy sauce

2   tablespoons honey

1   teaspoon garlic powder

1   teaspoon ground ginger

¼   teaspoon ground black pepper

2   tablespoons olive oil

1   pound chicken breast tenders

1   bag (16 ounces) frozen Oriental vegetables

There's no chopping at all in this easy and speedy skillet-fry.

LET'S BEGIN Whisk together the pineapple juice and cornstarch in a small bowl until blended. Whisk in the soy sauce, honey, garlic powder, ginger, and pepper and set aside.

STIR-FRY Heat the oil in a large skillet over medium-high heat. Stir-fry the chicken for 8 minutes, or until the juices run clear. Transfer to a plate and keep warm.

TOSS & SERVE Pour the reserved juice mixture into the skillet and stir over medium heat for 5 minutes, or until it boils. Return the chicken to the skillet and stir in the vegetables. Stir-fry for 7 minutes, or until vegetables are tender.

> *Makes 4 servings*
>
> *Per serving: 290 calories, 30g protein, 21g carbohydrates, 8g fat, 1g saturated fat, 66mg cholesterol, 1,755mg sodium*

Mediterranean Chicken Breasts

SuperQuick

TENDERS WITH LEMON-SPINACH RICE

Prep **10 MINUTES**   *Cook* **16 MINUTES**

1   tablespoon butter or margarine

1   pound chicken breast tenders

2   garlic cloves, minced

1½   cups instant brown rice

1   can (14½ ounces) chicken broth

1   tablespoon lemon juice

2   teaspoons grated lemon zest

2   cups loosely packed spinach leaves, cut into thin strips

Start this dish with the pick-of-the-chick: those juicy delicate tenders that cook in only 6 minutes. Use prewashed baby spinach, and speed up the preparation even more.

LET'S BEGIN Melt the butter in a large skillet over medium heat, then add the chicken tenders and garlic. Cook, turning, for 6 minutes or until the chicken is golden brown and the juices run clear. Transfer to a plate and keep warm.

COOK IT QUICK Add all of the remaining ingredients except the spinach to the skillet and bring to a boil over high heat. Cover and reduce the heat to low. Cook for 10 minutes, or until the liquid is absorbed.

TOSS & SERVE Add the spinach to the skillet and toss to mix well. Place on a large platter and top with the chicken.

Makes 4 servings

Per serving: 280 calories, 30g protein, 27g carbohydrates, 6g fat, 2g saturated fat, 74mg cholesterol, 525mg sodium

CHICKEN WITH DIJON CRÈME

Prep **5 MINUTES** *Cook* **22 MINUTES**

Soy milk, Dijon mustard, and sour cream make a creamy, ever-so-elegant sauce for delicious boneless breasts.

1	tablespoon olive oil
4	boneless, skinless chicken breast halves (about 1¼ pounds)
¼	cup finely chopped onion
1	cup plain soy milk
1	tablespoon Dijon mustard
¼	teaspoon salt
1½	teaspoons lemon juice
¾	teaspoon cornstarch
2	tablespoons sour cream
1	tablespoon chopped fresh dill

Ground black pepper

LET'S BEGIN Heat the oil in a large skillet over medium-high heat. Cook the chicken and onion, turning, for 6 minutes, or until the chicken is golden brown. Stir in the soy milk.

COOK IT QUICK Cover and cook over medium-low heat for 10 minutes, or until the chicken juices run clear. With a slotted spoon, transfer the chicken to a plate and keep warm.

MAKE IT SAUCY Whisk the mustard and salt into the soy milk and cook until bubbly. Whisk together the lemon juice and cornstarch in a cup until blended, then whisk into the soy milk. Stir in the sour cream and dill. Heat, stirring constantly, just until smooth (do not let boil), then season with pepper. Add the chicken and cook for 2 minutes.

Makes 4 servings

Per serving: 210 calories, 30g protein, 4g carbohydrates, 8g fat, 2g saturated fat, 80mg cholesterol, 350mg sodium

On the Menu

Double the recipe and stage a dinner party. This meal's quick but oh-so-impressive!

Chicken with
Dijon Crème

White & Wild Rice Pilaf

Mesclun with Green
Apples & Scallions
White Wine Vinaigrette

Hot Popovers

Raspberry Sorbet
Topped with
Fresh Blackberries

SuperQuick
CHICKEN ROMANO

Prep **5 MINUTES**   *Cook* **25 MINUTES**

1   cup long-grain white rice

1   tablespoon vegetable oil

1   pound boneless, skinless chicken breast halves, cut into ¼-inch-wide strips

1   medium onion, chopped

1   teaspoon Italian seasoning

1   can (14½ ounces) Italian-style stewed or diced tomatoes, undrained

½   cup grated Parmesan cheese

Here's a quick-toss skillet dish with fabulous Italian flavors and one big difference from what you'd find in Rome: it comes together in minutes instead of hours.

LET'S BEGIN Prepare the rice according to package directions and keep warm.

BROWN IT Heat the oil in a large skillet over medium-high heat. Add the chicken, onion, and Italian seasoning. Cook, stirring, for 5 minutes, or until the chicken is golden brown and the onion softens.

SPRINKLE & SERVE Add the rice and tomatoes and cook for 3 minutes, or until heated through. Sprinkle with the Parmesan.

Makes 4 servings

Per serving: 421 calories, 35g protein, 44g carbohydrates, 11g fat, 3g saturated fat, 80mg cholesterol, 964mg sodium

SuperQuick

CHICKEN IN BRANDIED CREAM

Prep **5 MINUTES**   *Cook* **15 MINUTES**

Here's a pasta sauce that takes chicken to an elegant level, reminiscent of the creamy sauces of France. Serve with fresh asparagus spears and orange sorbet for dessert.

8	ounces angel-hair pasta
1	pound boneless, skinless chicken breast halves
1	tablespoon olive oil
½	cup dried cherries
¼	cup brandy
2	scallions, sliced
2	teaspoons hot pepper sauce
1	teaspoon salt
1	cup heavy cream

LET'S BEGIN Cook the pasta according to package directions. Drain and keep warm. Cut the chicken into 1-inch-wide strips.

COOK IT QUICK Heat the oil in a large skillet over medium-high heat. Sauté the chicken for 6 minutes, or until it browns. Stir in the cherries, brandy, scallions, hot pepper sauce, and salt and bring to a boil.

SIMMER LOW Reduce the heat and simmer, stirring occasionally, for 5 minutes, or until the flavors blend. Stir in the cream and cook for 1 minute, or until heated through. Toss with the pasta.

Makes 4 servings

Per serving: 661 calories, 35g protein, 57g carbohydrates, 28g fat, 15g saturated fat, 148mg cholesterol, 700mg sodium

Cooking Basics

HOW MANY BIRDS FEED THE ROOST & HOW LONG DO I COOK THEM?

Here's a rule of thumb for **how much uncooked chicken to buy:**
• 7 to 8 ounces of bone-in chicken parts for 1 serving
• 5 ounces of boneless chicken for 1 serving
• a 3½-pound whole chicken to feed 4 people

To get 3 cups of cooked meat, buy:
• Buy a 3-pound Deli-roasted chicken
• Cook 1½ pounds boneless chicken pieces

Here's how to tell when the bird is done:
• Insert an instant-read thermometer into the thickest part of the thigh without touching the bone. When the thermometer reaches 180°F, it's time to take the bird out of the oven. Let the bird stand for 15 minutes before slicing, to firm up the juices.
• Another test is to pierce the thickest part of the thigh with a fork. When the juices run clear, not pink, the bird is done.
• Check the stuffing too. When the center of the stuffing reaches 165°F, it has cooked perfectly.

Quick Stir-fry Salad, page 47

Fast & Fresh

Fresh ingredients that you can put together fast to make great-tasting dishes—that's what the recipes in this chapter are all about. Toss up everyone's favorite chicken salad with a spice of curry, a dash of honey mustard, or a handful of fresh strawberries. Learn the secrets of stir-frying chicken successfully every time, plus ways to cut down your slicing and dicing time, too. Enjoy serving up an antipasto salad one night, a fusion stir-fry another, and a southwestern grilled salad still another. Whatever the season, you'll discover how healthy, fast, easy, and delicious these quick-cooking creations with chicken can be for a simple supper or an evening with friends.

CHICKEN WALDORF SALAD

Prep **10 MINUTES**   *Cook* **10 MINUTES**

1   pound boneless, skinless chicken breast halves

Salt and ground black pepper

¾   cup water

1   red apple

1   crisp green apple

¾   cup sliced celery

2   cartons (6 ounces each) orange or vanilla nonfat yogurt

½   cup nonfat mayonnaise

¼   cup California walnuts, chopped

4   cups shredded lettuce

Oscar Tschirky of the Waldorf-Astoria Hotel in New York City first created this salad in 1893, using only apples, celery, and mayonnaise. By 1928, walnuts had been added.

LET'S BEGIN Sprinkle the chicken with salt and pepper. Bring the water to a boil in a medium skillet over high heat. Add the chicken. Cover, reduce the heat, and simmer for 8 minutes, or until the juices run clear. Drain and cool. Cut the chicken into 1-inch chunks and transfer to a large bowl.

TOSS IT UP Core the apples (do not peel) and cut into 1-inch chunks. Add to the chicken with all of the remaining ingredients except the lettuce. If you wish, chill up to several hours. Toss to mix and serve on lettuce.

Makes 6 servings

Per serving: 204 calories, 21g protein, 19g carbohydrates, 4g fat, 1g saturated fat, 44mg cholesterol, 310mg sodium

EASY CAESAR SALAD

Prep **10 MINUTES**

2   cans (5 ounces each) chunk chicken breast, drained and flaked

4   cups torn romaine lettuce

1   cup cherry, pear, or grape tomatoes, halved

1   medium red onion, cut into rings

½   cup Caesar salad dressing

Parmesan cheese shavings

As the story goes, restaurant owner Caesar Cardini first served this salad to several Hollywood stars at his restaurant in Tijuana, Mexico in 1924. It received rave reviews! Try our quick-to-fix variation of the original, which uses chicken right from a can.

LET'S BEGIN Combine the chicken, lettuce, tomatoes, and onion in a large serving bowl. If not serving immediately, cover and refrigerate.

TOSS IT UP Add the dressing to the salad and toss to mix well. Sprinkle with Parmesan shavings.

Makes 4 servings

Per serving: 260 calories, 16g protein, 7g carbohydrates, 19g fat, 4g saturated fat, 36mg cholesterol, 657mg sodium

Chicken Waldorf Salad

SOUTHWESTERN GRILLED SALAD

Prep **10 MINUTES** *Grill* **20 MINUTES**

1	pound boneless, skinless chicken breast halves
8	cups loosely packed mixed baby salad greens
1	cup tomato wedges
½	cup canned black beans, rinsed and drained
¼	cup sliced scallions
½	cup shredded Mexican-style four-cheese blend

Take a trip to the sunny Southwest, where they love to grill. Olé!

LET'S BEGIN Oil the grill rack. Preheat the grill or a ridged grill pan. Grill the chicken, turning once, for 20 minutes, or until the juices run clear. Cut the chicken into strips.

TOP & SERVE Line a large platter with the salad greens. Top with the chicken, tomato, beans, and scallions. Sprinkle with the cheese. Serve with ranch dressing and salsa, if you like.

Makes 4 servings

Per serving: 230 calories, 32g protein, 9g carbohydrates, 6 fat, 3g saturated fat, 78mg cholesterol, 290mg sodium

HONEY-MUSTARD CHICKEN SALAD

Prep **10 MINUTES**

1	package (9 ounces) grilled chicken breast strips
¼	cup chopped pecans
2	scallions, sliced
1	large apple, such as Granny Smith, peeled cored, and cut into 1-inch chunks
1	rib celery, chopped
½	cup honey Dijon dressing

Here's the fastest salad in town, all from a package of grilled chicken.

TOSS IT UP Combine all of the ingredients in a serving bowl and toss until mixed well. Serve or cover and refrigerate.

Makes 4 servings

Per serving: 240 calories, 14g protein, 19g carbohydrates, 13g fat, 1g saturated fat, 45mg cholesterol, 935mg sodium

SuperQuick
STRAWBERRY-PATCH SALAD

Prep **20 MINUTES**

Any time is strawberry time! Mix up this wonderful curry-scented chicken salad. To make it even faster, use leftover chicken or pick up some precooked chicken at the market.

½   cup reduced-fat mayonnaise

2   tablespoons chopped chutney

1   teaspoon grated lime zest

1   tablespoon lime juice

1   teaspoon curry powder

1   teaspoon salt

2   cups diced cooked chicken

1   cup sliced celery

¼   cup chopped red onion

1½   pints strawberries, hulled

Lettuce leaves

LET'S BEGIN Mix the first 6 ingredients together in a large bowl. Stir in the chicken, celery, and onion. If you wish, cover and refrigerate up to several hours.

SLICE & SERVE Slice 1 pint of the strawberries and gently toss with the chicken mixture. Line a platter or plates with lettuce. Mound the chicken salad in the center and garnish with the remaining whole strawberries.

Makes 4 servings

Per serving: 289 calories, 22g protein, 25g carbohydrates, 12g fat, 2g saturated fat, 69mg cholesterol, 970mg sodium

Chicken Antipasto Salad

SuperQuick

CHICKEN ANTIPASTO SALAD

Prep **15 MINUTES**

12	cups loosely packed mixed baby salad greens (14 ounces)
1	jar (16 ounces) pepperoncini, drained
6	ounces cooked Italian-style chicken breast strips
½	cup pitted ripe olives
1	cup shredded mozzarella
1	cup grape tomatoes
½	cup Italian pesto dressing

This easy-to-fix salad is fantastic! Throw it together in minutes, or make it several hours ahead, if you like. "Dress," mix, and serve.

LET'S BEGIN Put the salad greens into a large salad bowl. Add all of the remaining ingredients and mix well. If not serving immediately, cover and refrigerate.

TOSS & SERVE Right before serving, add the dressing and toss to mix well.

> *Makes 6 servings*
>
> *Per serving: 247 calories, 16g protein, 9g carbohydrates, 16g fat, 5g saturated fat, 42mg cholesterol, 1,523mg sodium*

SuperQuick

QUICK STIR-FRY SALAD

Prep **10 MINUTES**   *Cook* **11 MINUTES**

1	tablespoon oil
1¼	pounds boneless, skinless chicken breast halves, cut into strips
3	cups sliced vegetables, such as bell peppers, carrots, mushrooms, and broccoli florets
8	cups loosely packed mixed baby salad greens (10 ounces)
½	cup Italian dressing
2	tablespoons soy sauce

Vary this warm salad by tossing with new dressing—Italian one day, red wine vinaigrette another, balsamic still another.

LET'S BEGIN Heat the oil in a wok or large skillet over medium-high heat for 1 minute.

STIR-FRY Add the chicken and stir-fry for 5 minutes, or until golden. Stir in the vegetables and stir-fry for 5 minutes longer, or until crisp-tender. Transfer to a large salad bowl. Add the salad greens to the bowl and mix well.

TOSS & SERVE Whisk together the dressing and the soy sauce in a cup, then drizzle over the salad-vegetable mixture. Toss to combine.

> *Makes 4 servings*
>
> *Per serving: 373 calories, 36g protein, 13g carbohydrates, 20g fat, 3g saturated fat, 82mg cholesterol, 871mg sodium*

CHICKEN, BROCCOLI, & PINEAPPLE STIR-FRY

Prep **15 MINUTES**   *Cook* **13 MINUTES**

½   pound boneless, skinless chicken breast halves

2   teaspoons vegetable oil

1   medium onion, sliced

1   tablespoon chopped, peeled fresh ginger

2   garlic cloves, minced

1   cup chicken broth

¼   cup soy sauce

1   tablespoon cornstarch

½   teaspoon anise seeds, crushed

¼   teaspoon ground cinnamon

2   cups broccoli florets

1   large red bell pepper, cut into chunks

2   cups fresh pineapple chunks

Fresh pineapple is the secret to this quick stir-fry; it adds a great sweet-and-sour flavor to the chicken and veggies. Make a pot of steamed rice, and your dinner's ready.

LET'S BEGIN Cut the chicken into ½-inch-wide strips. Heat the oil in a wok or large nonstick skillet over medium-high heat. Stir-fry the chicken for 5 minutes, or until golden brown. Transfer to a bowl and keep warm. Add the onion, ginger, and garlic to the wok or skillet and stir-fry for 2 minutes.

MAKE IT SAUCY Stir the broth, soy sauce, cornstarch, anise seeds, and cinnamon in a cup. Add to the wok or skillet and stir-fry for 2 minutes, or until the sauce thickens and boils. Add the broccoli and bell pepper. Cover and cook for 2 to 3 minutes, until the broccoli is crisp-tender.

SERVE Add the pineapple and chicken. Stir-fry 1 minute longer, or until heated through.

Makes 4 servings
Per serving: 185 calories, 18g protein, 21g carbohydrates, 4g fat, 1g saturated fat, 33mg cholesterol, 1,275mg sodium

---

Cook to Cook

HOW CAN I WHIP UP A MARINADE THAT WORKS FAST?

❝I've found that *seasonings in quick marinades must be very concentrated,* like using three cloves of garlic instead of one.

Add some salt or acid to the marinade. Buttermilk, lemon juice, or wine work well with chicken. They tenderize and flavor at the same time.

Let chicken stay in a strong marinade only an hour in the refrigerator. If it stands in a marinade too long, it may become mushy or stringy.❞

SuperQuick

CHICKEN PRIMAVERA

Prep **13 MINUTES**   *Cook* **17 MINUTES**

4	tablespoons butter or margarine
1	pound boneless, skinless chicken breast halves, cut into strips
8	ounces asparagus, cut into 1-inch lengths
2	leeks, white part only, trimmed, rinsed, and cut into ½-inch-thick slices
1	cup sliced white mushrooms
1	red bell pepper, cut into strips
4	tablespoons dry vermouth or water
16	ounces fresh fettuccine
½	cup heavy cream
1	tablespoon Dijon mustard
¼	cup grated Parmesan cheese
¼	teaspoon ground black pepper

Leeks are notorious for having sand and grit between their layers. To clean them, slice into ½-inch pieces and splash into a bowl of cold water. Swish and strain them out with a slotted spoon.

LET'S BEGIN Bring a large pot of salted water to a boil. Meanwhile, melt the butter in a large skillet over medium heat. Sauté the chicken for 10 minutes. Transfer to a bowl and keep warm.

TOSS IT Add the asparagus, leeks, mushrooms, bell pepper, and 2 tablespoons of the vermouth to the skillet. Sauté for 2 minutes. Add to the chicken in the bowl.

MAKE IT SAUCY Cook the pasta in the boiling water for 2 minutes, or until al dente. Drain and keep hot. Add the cream, the remaining vermouth, and the mustard to the skillet, whisking, until the sauce bubbles. Add the Parmesan, black pepper, and chicken and vegetables and cook for 2 minutes, or until hot. Serve over the fettuccine.

Makes 6 servings
Per serving: 516 calories, 30g protein, 50g carbohydrates, 21g fat, 12g saturated fat, 173mg cholesterol, 250mg sodium

SuperQuick

ASIAN COLESLAW

Prep **10 MINUTES**

1 cup shredded cooked chicken

1 package (8 ounces) coleslaw mix

½ small red onion, thinly sliced

¼ cup chopped fresh cilantro

¾ cup prepared Asian salad dressing

½ cup crispy chow mein noodles or chopped salted roasted peanuts

4 fresh cilantro sprigs

If you don't have prepared Asian salad dressing on hand, mix up a few tablespoons of rice or white wine vinegar, a few teaspoons of toasted sesame or peanut oil, and a teaspoon of soy sauce. Taste and adjust for seasonings.

LET'S BEGIN Mix the chicken, coleslaw, onion, and cilantro together in a medium bowl.

TOSS IT Drizzle with the dressing and toss well.

TOP & SERVE Top with chow mein noodles and garnish with the cilantro sprigs.

Makes 4 servings

Per serving: 210 calories, 13g protein, 22g carbohydrates, 4g fat, 1g saturated fat, 30mg cholesterol, 1,131mg sodium

GRILLED CHICKEN, GRAPEFRUIT, & ARUGULA SALAD

Prep **15 MINUTES**   *Grill* **10 MINUTES**

½   cup Grapefruit Vinaigrette (see recipe)

1   pound boneless, skinless chicken breast halves

4   ounces loosely packed trimmed arugula (4 cups)

1   cup loosely packed fresh mint leaves

1½   cups grapefruit sections, preferably ruby red (about 2 large grapefruit)

4   ounces feta cheese, crumbled (½ cup)

4   ounces Niçoise olives

To cut perfect grapefruit sections, remove the peel and pith of the grapefruit with a paring knife. Then, holding the grapefruit in your hand, cut down directly next to the membranes on both sides of each section and pop out the fruit.

LET'S BEGIN Prepare the Grapefruit Vinaigrette. Preheat the grill to medium or preheat the broiler. Grill (or broil) the chicken, turning once, for 10 minutes, or until the juices run clear. Cut into 1-inch chunks.

FIX IT FAST Decoratively arrange the arugula and mint leaves on a large platter or on 4 plates. Top with the chicken and grapefruit and sprinkle with the feta and olives.

DRIZZLE & SERVE Drizzle the salad with the vinaigrette right before serving.

GRAPEFRUIT VINAIGRETTE

Whisk together 1 cup chilled grapefruit juice (preferably fresh), ½ cup balsamic vinaigrette dressing, and 1 teaspoon grated grapefruit zest. Store in the refrigerator in a covered container. Makes 1½ cups.

Makes 4 servings
Per serving: 314 calories, 32g protein, 14g carbohydrates, 15g fat, 6g saturated fat, 91mg cholesterol, 718mg sodium

ASIAN WALNUT CHICKEN

Prep **15 MINUTES**   *Cook* **13 MINUTES**

1   cup long-grain white rice

½   cup chopped California walnuts

1   can (14½ ounces) reduced-sodium chicken broth

3   tablespoons cornstarch

1   tablespoon curry powder

1   pound boneless, skinless chicken breast halves, cut into 1-inch cubes

2   medium carrots, thinly sliced on the diagonal

1   small red bell pepper, cut into thin strips

4   scallions, cut on the diagonal into 1-inch lengths

Salt

Curry powder, chicken, and walnuts are a fabulous combination in this quick stir-fry. Be sure to use fresh curry powder.

LET'S BEGIN Cook the rice according to package directions and keep warm. Cook the walnuts in a dry skillet over medium-high heat for 1 minute, or until walnuts are slightly toasted. Whisk the broth, cornstarch, and curry powder together in a medium bowl.

SAUTÉ IT QUICK Coat a large nonstick skillet with cooking spray and set over medium-high heat. Add the chicken and sauté for 5 minutes, or until golden brown. Stir in the carrots, bell pepper, and scallions and sauté for 2 minutes.

SIMMER & SERVE Stir in the broth mixture and bring to a boil. Cover and reduce heat to medium-low. Cook, stirring, for 4 minutes, or until the chicken juices run clear. Season with salt. Serve over rice and sprinkle with walnuts.

Makes 6 servings
Per serving: 292 calories, 23g protein, 33g carbohydrates, 8g fat, 1g saturated fat, 44mg cholesterol, 188mg sodium

FUSION STIR-FRY
Prep **15 MINUTES**   *Cook* **15 MINUTES**

1   box (6 ounces) rice pilaf

2   tablespoons olive oil

1   teaspoon chili-garlic
      paste or sauce

1   pound thin asparagus,
      cut diagonally into
      1½-inch lengths

1   red bell pepper, cut into
      thin strips

¼   cup sliced scallions

1   package (10 ounces)
      cooked lemon pepper–
      seasoned carved chicken
      breasts

2   tablespoons thinly sliced
      fresh basil

2   teaspoons cornstarch

1   cup chicken broth

Fusion food is a mix of cultures and flavors—and here's a prime example. The recipe combines both Asian and Mediterranean flavors with an Asian cooking technique.

LET'S BEGIN   Prepare pilaf according to package directions. Keep warm. Meanwhile, heat oil and chili-garlic paste in a wok or large nonstick skillet over medium-high heat.

STIR-FRY   Add the asparagus, bell pepper, and scallions and stir-fry for 2 to 3 minutes. Add the chicken and basil and stir-fry 1 to 2 minutes longer, or until heated through.

MAKE IT SAUCY   Meanwhile, whisk the cornstarch and broth together in a cup until blended. Add the sauce to the center of the wok all at once and stir-fry for 1 minute, or until the sauce thickens and boils. Serve over the rice pilaf.

Makes 4 servings

Per serving: 373 calories, 30g protein, 40g carbohydrates, 11g fat, 2g saturated fat, 60mg cholesterol, 923mg sodium

SuperQuick
ORANGE TERIYAKI STIR-FRY

Prep **10 MINUTES**   *Cook* **10 MINUTES**

1   package (24 ounces) teriyaki boneless, skinless chicken breasts

1   tablespoon vegetable oil

½   pound fresh or frozen sugar snap peas

⅓   cup orange juice

¼   teaspoon red pepper flakes

¼   tablespoon salt

3   tablespoons sesame seeds, toasted

Hot cooked angel-hair pasta (optional)

Make this fast stir-fry even faster by substituting precooked chicken strips for the fresh. Just stir them in during the last minute of cooking. Cook up fresh pasta rather than dried.

LET'S BEGIN Cut the chicken into strips. Heat the oil in a wok or large nonstick skillet over medium-high heat.

STIR-FRY Stir-fry the chicken and snap peas for 4 to 5 minutes, or until the chicken juices run clear. Add all of the remaining ingredients and stir-fry for 1 minute, or until heated through. Serve over pasta, if desired.

Makes 4 servings

Per serving: 400 calories, 56g protein, 11g carbohydrates, 13g fat, 3g saturated fat, 145mg cholesterol, 332mg sodium

Cooking Basics

3 SIMPLE STEPS TO A FASTER STIR-FRY

#1 SMART START-UP
Slice and dice the foods to be cooked at the same time similar size, so they will be done at the same time. If the recipe doesn't have a thickened sauce and you want one, toss meat or seafood in a little cornstarch. For extra flavor, marinate in soy sauce.

#2 FAST FRY
Choose an oil with a high smoking point that cooks without burning easily, such as peanut, canola, or soybean. Before adding the food, warm the empty wok or large nonstick skillet over high heat to get hot, then glaze it fast with a swish of oil. Brown the meat or seafood first, push it up the sides, then add the vegetables and aromatics. Keep moving the food until the vegetables are crisp-tender.

#3 SAUCE & SEASON IT UP!
Push the ingredients up the sides. Whisk up the sauce with seasonings (pepper flakes, sugar, soy sauce). Pour the sauce into the center of the wok all at once and stir-fry 1 to 2 minutes until hot and sauce glazes and thickens.

SuperQuick
CHICKEN & BLACK BEAN SALAD
Prep **15 MINUTES**   *Cook* **12 MINUTES**

2   tablespoons vegetable oil

1   medium red onion, chopped

1   pound boneless, skinless chicken breast halves, cut into ¾-inch chunks

1   can (16 ounces) black beans, rinsed and drained

1   medium tomato, diced

½   cup pepperoncini, seeded and chopped plus additional whole peppers

3   tablespoons chopped fresh parsley

2   tablespoons cider vinegar

1   teaspoon salt

1   teaspoon hot pepper sauce

Lettuce leaves

Black beans (turtle beans) are popular ingredients in Caribbean dishes. Use canned ones and supper's ready in 25 minutes.

LET'S BEGIN Heat 1 tablespoon oil in a large skillet over medium heat. Sauté the onion for 5 minutes. Put in a bowl.

FLASH INTO THE PAN Add the remaining 1 tablespoon oil to the skillet. Increase the heat to medium-high and sauté the chicken for 5 minutes, or until golden brown and the juices run clear. Add to the onion in the bowl.

TOSS & SERVE Add all of the remaining ingredients except the lettuce and whole peppers. Setve salad on lettuce leaves and garnish with the whole peppers.

Makes 4 servings

Per serving: 346 calories, 35g protein, 27g carbohydrates, 11g fat, 1g saturated fat, 72mg cholesterol, 1,162mg sodium

Cooking Basics

COOK DRIED BEANS IN HALF THE TIME

Nothing can beat opening a can of beans when you're in a hurry. But cooking your own dried beans adds more flavor to the dish. Soak beans in a quarter of the time (one hour instead of four) by using this fast quick-soak method. Here's how: Rinse the beans in a colander, place in a pot, and cover with water. Bring to a boil and cook for 3 minutes. Remove from the heat, cover tightly, and let stand 1 hour.

Drain and rinse the beans, then cover with fresh cold water and cook as directed on the package or in your recipe. Add salt only during the last 15 minutes, after the beans are tender. If added earlier, salt toughens beans and increases the cooking time. Freeze the drained beans in quart containers if you wish. Whenever a recipe calls for beans, just thaw—they're ready to toss right in!

SPEED-DRY YOUR GREENS!

Even if the bag touts prewashed, it's a good idea to freshen the greens with one more swish in the sink. Dry greens thoroughly (they'll stay crisp longer). Use a salad spinner, or paper towels. When greens are dry, the salad dressing not only adheres better but also tastes better since it is not diluted with water.

KEEP THEM CRISP

Wrap washed dry greens in a paper towel then slide them into a plastic bag. Punch out a few holes, or use a perforated bag. Push out any excess air before sealing and store in your refrigerator's crisper drawer.

GREENS FOR A CROWD

For large amounts of salads, toss washed greens into a clean white pillowcase. Push out the excess air and tie with string. Step outside and swing the pillowcase around and around. The centrifugal force will "magically" dry your greens Refrigerate until serving time.

SuperQuick
WISCONSIN CHEESE & GRILLED CHICKEN SALAD

Prep **20 MINUTES**

For the best flavor, make this fast salad with warm chicken. If you're using leftover chicken, just heat it gently in the oven or in the microwave.

3	cups grilled chicken breasts, sliced
1	cup red wine vinegar and oil salad dressing
1	tablespoon honey
1	tablespoon whole-grain Dijon mustard
4	cups torn mixed salad greens, such as iceberg, red leaf, and chicory
2	cups shredded purple kale or red cabbage
1½	cups drained canned whole corn kernels
2	medium onions, very thinly sliced
1½	cups shredded Colby cheese (6 ounces)

LET'S BEGIN Toss the first 4 ingredients together in a medium bowl.

TOSS IT Combine the remaining ingredients in a large serving bowl and toss until mixed well.

SERVE Right before serving, add the chicken along with any dressing remaining in the bowl to the greens. Gently toss to mix well.

Makes 6 servings

Per serving: 378 calories, 31g protein, 29g carbohydrates, 12g fat, 6g saturated fat, 86mg cholesterol, 1,251mg sodium

Chicken Taco with Corn Salsa, page 79

Bread Board

Take your pick of the many breads in the bakeries today, or bake your own. Poach, grill, or roast up some chicken, then slice or dice it. Slather on some sandwich spread, sprinkle on some seasonings, pile on the fillings, and stack up the sandwiches. There are so many favorites to choose from here. Try the Garden Salad Sub that's super-quick to fix, thanks to ready-to-eat grilled chicken strips…or the Chicken & Avocado Wraps with lots of Mexican spice. There are plenty of pizzas—in the styles of Santa Fe, Tex-Mex, and even down on the ranch. However you wrap them, grill them, or stuff them, these sandwiches bring new flavors to supper—in a matter of minutes.

SuperQuick

CHERRY-CHICKEN CROISSANTS

Prep **20 MINUTES**

2 cups cubed cooked chicken

½ cup dried tart cherries

3 scallions, sliced

½ cup mayonnaise

¼ cup plain yogurt

1 tablespoon lemon juice

Ground black pepper

2 large or 4 small croissants

Chopped fresh parsley

Lettuce leaves

Here's a new twist for chicken salad—dried cherries, yogurt, and a splash of fresh lemon juice. Make in the morning and chill, then just stuff into flaky croissants. Supper's ready!

LET'S BEGIN Combine the chicken, cherries, and scallions in a large bowl.

FIX IT FAST Stir the mayonnaise, yogurt, and lemon juice together in a small bowl and season with pepper. Stir into the chicken mixture until well combined. If you wish, cover and refrigerate for up to 2 hours.

STUFF & SERVE Split the croissants horizontally, cutting almost but not completely through. Stuff each with some chicken salad, sprinkle with parsley, and top with a lettuce leaf.

Makes 2 servings

Per serving: 880 calories, 52g protein, 77g carbohydrates, 40g fat, 13g saturated fat, 184mg cholesterol, 1,079mg sodium

OPEN-FACED SANDWICHES WITH ORANGE-WALNUT MAYONNAISE

Prep **15 MINUTES**   Cook **8 MINUTES**

When you want dressed-up sandwiches, try these. If possible, buy the French baguette the same day, cut diagonally with a serrated knife into slices about ¾-inch thick.

2	teaspoons ground cumin
2	teaspoons paprika
2	skinless, boneless chicken breast halves (about 10 ounces)
¾	cup nonfat mayonnaise
½	cup chopped California walnuts
2	tablespoons grated orange zest
1	tablespoon chopped fresh mint
16	½-inch-thick diagonal slices French baguette
16	small watercress or fresh parsley sprigs

LET'S BEGIN Mix the cumin and paprika together and rub over the chicken. Coat a medium nonstick skillet with cooking spray. Cook the chicken over medium-high heat for 4 minutes on each side, or until the juices run clear.

LET IT REST Let the chicken cool, then cut each piece on the diagonal into 8 slices (make them approximately the same thickness as the bread slices). Set aside.

STACK & SERVE Stir the mayonnaise, walnuts, orange zest, and mint together in a small bowl. Spread each slice of bread with a generous tablespoon of the walnut-mayonnaise. Top with a slice of chicken and a watercress sprig. Arrange on a platter and serve.

Makes 4 servings

Per serving: 499 calories, 28g protein, 62g carbohydrates, 14g fat, 2g saturated fat, 41mg cholesterol, 1,020mg sodium

Cooking Basics

CHOPPING BOARD SAFETY

PICK THE BEST BOARD
It's a fact: Chopping boards make slicing, chopping, and dicing easier and faster. Wooden boards are gentler on your knives than plastic boards. This means they save you sharpening time! Wooden boards also have natural enzymes that neutralize any bacteria coming their way. Just be sure to replace them if they develop cracks, where food can get caught. When using plastic boards, replace them if they become worn, warped, melted, or damaged.

KEEP MANY ON HAND
Take a tip from the chefs: Stock up on several chopping boards: one for chopping vegetables and nuts…a second board for slicing meats…still a third for cutting up poultry.

SCRUB 'EM CLEAN
Scrub and sanitize all boards with a paste of baking soda and water. **Remove odors and stains** from both wooden and plastic cutting boards with a paste of fresh lemon juice and salt. Rub it in, then rinse well. **Pop plastic boards into the dishwasher**—but never never use one to wash wooden boards. Just wipe those clean.

SuperQuick
GARDEN SALAD SUB
Prep **15 MINUTES**   *Bake* **5 MINUTES**

1   unsliced loaf Italian bread (about 1 pound)

⅓   cup plus 2 tablespoons Italian salad dressing

2   cups torn salad greens

1   package (6 ounces) grilled chicken breast strips

1   red bell pepper, chopped

1   package (4 ounces) crumbled feta cheese

This sandwich goes by many names—grinder, hoagie, bomber, wedge, or hero. Whatever you call it, it's fast and delicious!

LET'S BEGIN Preheat the oven to 350°F. Slice off the top ⅓ of the loaf. Pull out the soft insides, leaving ½-inch-thick shell. Brush the inside and top of the loaf with 2 tablespoons of the dressing. Place the bread on a cookie sheet, cut side up, and bake for 5 minutes, or until lightly toasted. Let cool.

STUFF & SERVE Toss all the remaining ingredients with the ⅓ cup dressing in a large bowl. Spoon into the bread shell, cover with the top, and cut diagonally into 2-inch-wide slices.

Makes 4 servings

Per serving: 590 calories, 28g protein, 63g carbohydrates, 24g fat, 7g saturated fat, 61mg cholesterol, 1,272mg sodium

---

SuperQuick
CHICKEN & PEPPER HEROES
Prep **15 MINUTES**   *Cook* **12 MINUTES**

1   pound boneless, skinless chicken breast halves

3   tablespoons olive oil

2   teaspoons hot pepper sauce

½   teaspoon salt

½   teaspoon ground cumin

1   large red bell pepper, cut into strips

1   large yellow or green bell pepper, cut into strips

½   cup crumbled feta cheese

4   hero rolls, split

These fast heroes are hot and hearty. Try bleu cheese for the feta.

LET'S BEGIN Cut chicken into strips. Heat 1 tablespoon of the oil in a large skillet over medium-high heat. Sauté the chicken for 6 minutes. Stir in the hot pepper sauce, salt, and cumin. Transfer the chicken mixture to a large bowl.

SAUTÉ & STUFF Heat the remaining oil in the same skillet over medium heat. Sauté the bell peppers for 5 minutes, or until crisp-tender. Add the peppers with the cheese to the chicken in the bowl and toss. Spoon onto the bottoms of the rolls, then cover with the tops.

Makes 4 servings

Per serving: 685 calories, 41g protein, 78g carbohydrates, 24g fat, 6g saturated fat, 82mg cholesterol, 1,272mg sodium

Garden Salad Sub

CHEESY CHICKEN BISCUIT SANDWICHES

Prep **15 MINUTES**   *Cook* **20 MINUTES**

1   **can (16.3 ounces) refrigerated buttermilk biscuits**

1   **pound boneless, skinless chicken breast halves, cut into 1-inch-wide strips**

⅛   **teaspoon salt**

⅛   **teaspoon ground black pepper**

8   **slices (¾ ounce each) American cheese, halved**

Turn biscuits into brunch or lunch. Stuff them with chicken, slide in a slice of cheese, and bake until hot and melted.

LET'S BEGIN Preheat the oven to 375°F. Separate the biscuit dough into 8 biscuits, gently pressing them down to form 5-inch rounds. Place them on a work surface.

STUFF Place the chicken strips in the middle of the dough rounds and sprinkle with salt and pepper. Top each with 2 half-slices of cheese. Fold two opposite sides of the biscuits into the center so they slightly overlap. Secure with wooden picks and place on a large cookie sheet.

INTO THE OVEN Bake the biscuit sandwiches for 18 to 20 minutes, until the chicken is cooked through. Remove the wooden picks.

Makes 8 servings

Per serving: 270 calories, 21g protein, 28g carbohydrates, 8g fat, 3g saturated fat, 47mg cholesterol, 813mg sodium

Cooking Basics

GREAT BREADS FOR FAST CHICKEN SANDWICHES

Artisan bakeries, bread boutiques, and supermarkets offer fabulous breads-to-go...a much faster alternative than baking bread yourself. Chicken makes the perfect filling.

FOCCACIA
A flat pizzalike dough, often baked with a brushing of olive oil and a sprinkling of fresh herbs and slivers of garlic or onion. Try it for grilled cheese and chicken-wiches. Or slice and serve with dipping oil.

CIABATTA
A slipper-shaped crusty bread, usually only about 4 inches thick. It's ideal for splitting and filling with sliced meats and chicken, coleslaw, and spicy dressings.

BAGUETTES
Long, skinny French loaves with golden crusty outsides, soft white insides. For a sandwich for 4 or more, leave the baguette whole, and split it horizontally.

BRIOCHE
Another French favorite that's often baked in a fluted mold with a topknot but also in sandwich buns and loaves. Ideal for chicken or shrimp salad.

LAVASH FLATBREADS
Another Middle-Eastern specialty that's ideal for roll-up wraps. Fill with thinly sliced meats, cheese, slaw, and thinly sliced vegetables before rolling up jelly-roll fashion.

BARBECUE & SLAW BUNS

Prep **10 MINUTES**   *Bake/Cook* **1 HOUR + 5 MINUTES**

3   bone-in chicken
     breast halves
     (about 1½ pounds)

BBQ SAUCE

1   cup ketchup

½   cup cider vinegar

¼   cup minced onion

2   garlic cloves, minced

2   teaspoons chili powder

½   teaspoons hot pepper
     sauce

SLAW

4   cups thinly sliced green
     cabbage

½   cup mayonnaise

2   tablespoons yellow
     mustard

1½   tablespoons cider
     vinegar

½   teaspoon celery seeds

¼   teaspoon salt

¼   teaspoon ground black
     pepper

4   hamburger buns, split

Most barbecue takes hours of long, slow simmering. These barbecue buns are a terrific, flavorful, and fast substitute. Save on the chopping time by buying a bag of presliced cabbage.

LET'S BEGIN Preheat the oven to 325°F. Put the chicken in a glass baking dish in a single layer. Whisk all of the sauce ingredients together in a small bowl and pour over the chicken, turning to coat. Turn the chicken, skin side up. Bake for 1 hour, or until the juices run clear. Set aside to cool slightly.

FIX IT FAST Meanwhile, stir all of the slaw ingredients together in a large bowl until mixed well. Set aside.

MAKE IT SAUCY Discard the chicken skin. Remove the meat from the bones and tear into shreds. Put into a large saucepan and stir in the barbecue sauce from the baking dish. Simmer over low heat, stirring, for 5 minutes, or until heated through. Serve barbecue and slaw in buns.

Makes 4 servings
Per serving: 530 calories, 29g protein, 47g carbohydrates, 27g fat, 5g saturated fat, 94mg cholesterol, 1,490mg sodium

SuperQuick
PITA POCKETS

Prep **15 MINUTES**   *Cook* **15 MINUTES**

4   boneless, skinless
       chicken breast halves
       (about 1¼ pounds)

¾   cup ranch dressing

1   tablespoon dill weed

2   tablespoons olive oil

1   cup sliced white
       mushrooms

1   cup thinly sliced onion

4   large pita breads, halved

1   cup shredded lettuce

Warm pita breads are faster and easier to stuff. Using tongs, warm them one-by-one for a few seconds over a gas burner.

LET'S BEGIN Place the chicken between plastic wrap and pound to an even thickness. Stir the ranch dressing and dill weed together in a cup and set aside.

FLASH IN THE PAN Heat 1 tablespoon of the oil in a large skillet over medium heat. Sauté the mushrooms and onion for 5 minutes, or until soft. Transfer to a plate. Heat the remaining 1 tablespoon oil. Cook the chicken for 5 minutes on each side, or until the juices run clear.

STUFF & SERVE Cut the chicken into strips. Stuff the pitas with lettuce, chicken, and mushrooms. Top with sauce.

Makes 4 servings

Per serving: 599 calories, 33g protein, 40g carbohydrates, 34g fat, 5g saturated fat, 77mg cholesterol, 853mg sodium

GRILLED CHEESY CHICKEN PITAS

Prep **5 MINUTES**   *Marinate* **30 MINUTES**   *Grill* **10 MINUTES**

¼ cup olive oil

2 tablespoons white wine vinegar

2 teaspoons chicken seasoning

½ teaspoon Italian seasoning

1 pound boneless, skinless chicken breasts

6 pita pockets

6 slices Monterey Jack or Muenster cheese

6 each: lettuce leaves and tomato slices

½ cup shredded carrots

To speed up the preparation of these pitas, buy precooked chicken and heat it up about fifteen seconds in the microwave.

LET'S BEGIN Combine the first 4 ingredients in a large self-closing plastic bag or glass dish. Add chicken and toss to coat. Refrigerate for 30 minutes or up to 1 hour for added flavor. Remove chicken from marinade and discard marinade.

FIRE UP THE GRILL Preheat grill and lightly grease grill rack. Grill chicken over medium-hot coals for 5 to 6 minutes per side or until juices run clear. Slice thinly.

STUFF & SERVE Layer the chicken in pita pockets. Top each with the cheese, lettuce, tomato, and carrots.

Makes 6 servings
Per serving: 458 calories, 32g protein, 33g carbohydrates, 21g fat, 7g saturated fat, 70mg cholesterol, 599mg sodium

SuperQuick
TEX-MEX ENCHILADAS

Prep **10 MINUTES**   *Bake* **20 MINUTES**

2 cups shredded cheese (half Cheddar, half Monterey Jack)

4 (7-inch) flour tortillas

2 cups cubed roasted chicken

Salt and ground black pepper

1 can (10 ounces) diced tomatoes

1 can (4½ ounces) chopped green chilies

1 cup fresh cilantro leaves

¼ cup sour cream

Here's supper, Texas style! Try substituting fire-roasted tomatoes.

LET'S BEGIN Preheat the oven to 350°F. Spray a 13x9-inch baking dish with cooking spray. Toss both cheeses. Rub tortillas with a little water. Warm in microwave 10 seconds.

STUFF & BAKE Top each tortilla with ¼ of chicken, season with salt and pepper, and sprinkle with ¼ of cheese. Roll up the tortillas and place seam side up in the dish. Cover and bake for 20 minutes, or until cheese melts. Meanwhile, heat tomatoes and chilies in a small saucepan, then stir in the cilantro. Serve the enchiladas with the sauce and sour cream.

Makes 4 servings
Per serving: 617 calories, 43g protein, 46g carbohydrates, 28g fat, 15g saturated fat, 119mg cholesterol, 1,119mg sodium

SuperQuick
PIZZA SANTA FE

Prep **10 MINUTES**   *Bake* **15 MINUTES**

1   prebaked pizza crust
    (12 inches)

½   cup guacamole

1   package (10 ounces)
    sliced cooked
    Southwest-style
    chicken breast

½   cup roasted red peppers,
    drained and sliced

2   cups shredded Pepper-
    Jack cheese (8 ounces)

*Pizzas take on Southwestern accents of peppers and spice.
Start with a prebaked crust, then make them even faster with
refrigerated guacamole and preshredded cheese.*

LET'S BEGIN Preheat the oven to 350°F. Place the pizza
crust on an oiled cookie sheet.

FIX IT FAST Spread the guacamole evenly over crust. Top
with the chicken and peppers and sprinkle with the cheese.

INTO THE OVEN Bake the pizza for 15 minutes, or until
the cheese bubbles and slightly browns. Cut pizza into wedges.

Makes 4 servings

*Per serving: 676 calories, 50g protein, 52g carbohydrates,
30g fat, 12g saturated fat, 119mg cholesterol, 1,257mg sodium*

SuperQuick
CHEESY CHICKEN PIZZA

Prep **15 MINUTES**   *Bake* **15 MINUTES**

1   package (10 ounces)
    refrigerated pizza dough

½   cup picante sauce

½   cup traditional pasta
    sauce

1   cup chopped cooked
    chicken

½   cup drained sliced pitted
    ripe olives

¼   cup sliced scallions

1   cup shredded mozzarella
    cheese (4 ounces)

*Everyone loves pizza, and this one is unusually good with its bright
Tex-Mex flavors. If you enjoy spicy food, quickly throw some
canned roasted chilies on top as well.*

LET'S BEGIN Preheat the oven to 425°F. Oil a 12-inch
pizza pan. Shape the dough into a 12-inch round on a lightly
floured surface. Place the dough in the pan and crimp the
edge to form a ½-inch rim.

FIX IT FAST Mix the picante and pasta sauces together in
a small bowl and spread over the dough to within ¼ inch of
the edge. Top with the remaining ingredients.

INTO THE OVEN Bake for 15 minutes, or until the crust
is golden and the cheese melts.

Makes 4 servings

*Per serving: 365 calories, 23g protein, 39g carbohydrates,
12g fat, 5g saturated fat, 52mg cholesterol, 1,124mg sodium*

Pizza Santa Fe

Ranch Pizza Pie

SuperQuick
RANCH PIZZA PIE
Prep **20 MINUTES**   *Bake* **10 MINUTES**

28	ounces refrigerated pizza dough
3	cloves garlic, minced
¼	cup olive oil
⅓	cup ranch dressing
2	cups mozzarella cheese, shredded (8 ounces)
1	cup Cheddar cheese, shredded (4 ounces)
1	medium onion, sliced
4	slices crumbled cooked bacon
1	cup diced cooked chicken
¾	cup chopped tomatoes

Ranch dressing makes a creamy base for this unusual pizza. Buy shredded cheese to speed up the preparation time.

LET'S BEGIN Shape the dough into a 16-inch round on a lightly floured surface. Place on a greased 16-inch pizza pan. Cover and let rise in a warm place until doubled in volume.

LAYER Preheat the oven to 425°F. Crimp the dough edge to form a rim. Mix the garlic and oil together and brush over the dough. Spread the ranch dressing on top and sprinkle with 1 cup of the mozzarella and ½ cup of the Cheddar. Layer the onion, bacon, chicken, and tomatoes on top, and sprinkle with the remaining mozzarella and Cheddar.

INTO THE OVEN Bake for 10 minutes, or until the crust is golden and the cheeses melt.

Makes 4 servings

Per serving: 1,121 calories, 48g protein, 100g carbohydrates, 59g fat, 20g saturated fat, 112mg cholesterol, 1,870mg sodium

SuperQuick
20-MINUTE PIZZA
Prep **10 MINUTES**   *Bake* **10 MINUTES**

1	cup chunky salsa, drained
1	baked pizza crust (12 inches)
1	package (10 ounces) mesquite-flavored sliced cooked chicken
1	cup shredded Cheddar cheese (4 ounces)
¼	cup drained sliced ripe olives

Thanks to a prebaked pizza crust and cooked chicken, this pizza's ready in 20 minutes flat.

LET'S BEGIN Preheat the oven to 450°F.

FIX IT FAST Spread the salsa over the pizza crust. Top with the chicken, Cheddar, and olives.

INTO THE OVEN Place pizza on a cookie sheet. Bake for 10 minutes, or until the crust is crisp and the cheese melts.

Makes 4 servings

Per serving: 580 calories, 41g protein, 54g carbohydrates, 22g fat, 8g saturated fat, 102mg cholesterol, 1,391mg sodium

CHICKEN & AVOCADO WRAPS

Prep **15 MINUTES**

1   pound cooked chicken

½   cup salsa

1   ripe avocado, halved, pitted, peeled, and chopped

¼   cup diced red onion

1½   teaspoons hot pepper sauce

¾   teaspoon salt

4   large flour tortillas

8   fresh cilantro sprigs (optional)

Warm up the tortillas one-by-one over a gas flame or in a 350°F oven (wrapped in foil) for 3 to 5 minutes. Then wrap, fill, fold and serve!

LET'S BEGIN Combine the chicken, salsa, avocado, onion, hot pepper sauce, and salt in a medium bowl.

ROLL THEM UP To assemble the wraps, spoon one-fourth of the chicken mixture down the middle of each tortilla and fold over the sides.

SERVE Garnish with cilantro sprigs, if you like.

Makes 4 servings

Per serving: 454 calories, 38g protein, 31g carbohydrates, 19g fat, 4g saturated fat, 101mg cholesterol, 850mg sodium

HONEY-OF-A-WRAP

Prep **10 MINUTES**   *Cook* **15 MINUTES**

1   tablespoon vegetable oil

1   pound boneless, skinless chicken breasts, cut into strips

1   large green bell pepper, cut into strips

1   large red bell pepper, cut into strips

3   tablespoons honey mustard

1   tablespoon lemon juice

4   large flour tortillas, warmed

Honey mustard provides a welcome flavor addition to these easy chicken wraps. Serve bowls of shredded lettuce and diced tomatoes.

LET'S BEGIN Heat the oil in a large skillet over medium-high heat. Sauté the chicken and red and green peppers for 5 minutes, or until juices run clear and the peppers are tender.

BUBBLE & STIR Stir in the mustard and lemon juice. Reduce the heat to low and simmer for 10 minutes, or until the chicken is cooked through.

ROLL THEM UP Spoon the chicken mixture down the middle of each tortilla and fold over sides.

Makes 4 servings

Per serving: 447 calories, 34g protein, 52g carbohydrates, 11g fat, 2g saturated fat, 66mg cholesterol, 548mg sodium

Chicken & Avocado Wraps

SuperQuick

CHICKEN RANCH WRAPS

Prep **15 MINUTES**

¼   **cup ranch dressing**

2   **large flour tortillas**

1   **cup diced cooked chicken**

4   **slices crisp-cooked bacon (optional)**

Lettuce leaves

Tomato slices

These wraps must be some of the fastest and tastiest around. Experiment with different salad dressings and see which is your favorite—they'll all be good.

LET'S BEGIN Spread the dressing over the tortillas.

FIX IT FAST Layer one-fourth of the chicken, bacon, lettuce, and tomato onto each tortilla.

ROLL 'EM UP Roll up the tortillas and serve.

Makes 2 servings

Per serving: 450 calories, 25g protein, 31g carbohydrates, 25g fat, 5g saturated fat, 64mg cholesterol, 651mg sodium

Cooking Basics

3 SIMPLE STEPS TO WRAP UP GREAT WRAPS

INSTANT WRAPPERS

The perfect wrappers are as close as your grocer. Look in the Mexican aisle or the refrigerator case for flour tortillas in the large burrito size. Generally they come in plain white, tomato red, and spinach green. Right before filling, warm up the wrappers. Pop them in the microwave on high for 10 seconds. Or hold one-at-a-time over a gas flame with long tongs, turning constantly, for about 1 minute, or until warm. Don't dry them out.

FAST FILLINGS

Almost anything that makes a great sandwich filling also makes wonderful wraps. Think contrasting textures, colors, flavorful fillings and lots of them.
The Parisian: Thin slices of baked ham (ask your butcher to help you out), Brie, shredded romaine, Dijon mustard, chopped gherkins.
The Venetian: Prosciutto, mozzarella, roasted red peppers, slivered basil, chopped red onion, balsamic vinaigrette.

Breakfast to Go: Fried egg, grilled Canadian bacon, whipped cream cheese with chives.
The Western: Sliced roasted beef, Monterey Jack with jalapeño peppers, crisp coleslaw.

WRAP IT QUICK

Layer up the fillings in the center, leaving about 2-inch border. Start with the driest ingredients first and end with the juiciest. Fold opposite ends toward the center, then roll from one side to the other.

CHICKEN TACOS WITH CORN SALSA

Prep **20 MINUTES**   *Cook* **35 MINUTES**

CORN SALSA

1   package (10 ounces) frozen whole-kernel corn

2   jalapeño peppers, seeded and minced

1   large tomato, diced

2   scallions, chopped

2   tablespoons chopped fresh cilantro

¼   cup lime juice

½   teaspoon salt

½   teaspoon ground black pepper

TACOS

1   whole chicken (3½ to 4 pounds) or chicken pieces

1   cup canned enchilada sauce

1   package (1¾ ounces) taco seasoning

8   corn tortillas

1   cup sour cream

1   cup shredded Cheddar cheese (4 ounces)

Following true Mexican tradition, these tacos are made with soft corn tortillas. To save time, buy a preroasted chicken or some precooked chicken breasts instead.

LET'S BEGIN Cook the corn according to package directions. Drain the corn, transfer to a medium bowl, and stir in the remaining salsa ingredients.

SIMMER LOW Remove the giblets and neck from the chicken and reserve for another use. Rinse the chicken inside and out and place in a large sauce pot with enough cold water to cover. Bring to a simmer over medium-high heat and cook for 20 minutes. Transfer the chicken to a cutting board and let cool. Remove the chicken meat from the bones and tear into bite-size pieces (you need about 2 cups). Discard the skin and bones. Stir the chicken, enchilada sauce, and taco seasoning together in a medium saucepan. Cook over low heat, stirring occasionally, for 15 minutes, or until the flavors blend.

SERVE 'EM UP Meanwhile, preheat the oven to 375°F. Wrap the tortillas in foil and warm them in the oven for 10 minutes. To make the tacos, spoon the corn and chicken mixture along the middle of the tortillas. Top with the salsa, sour cream, and cheese and fold the sides of the tortillas into the center to enclose the filling.

Makes 4 servings
Per serving: 665 calories, 45g protein, 56g carbohydrates, 30g fat, 15g saturated fat, 145mg cholesterol, 1,666mg sodium

Easy Chicken Stroganoff, page 99

Melting Pot Favorites

Your kitchen will travel the globe when you try our favorite chicken dishes from America's melting pot. They're cousins of authentic dishes, served for centuries by our international neighbors near and far. Start in Louisiana by putting chicken into the gumbo pot. Stop off in the Southwest to spice up the bird with chilies, then go on to Pennsylvania where they bake it with sauerkraut. Bring the taste of Italy to your supper table with a cacciatore, some saucy spaghetti, or a Mediterranean skillet. Travel on to the Orient for rice bowls, fried rice, and spicy Thai specialties. You'll soon find these recipes among your favorite ways to quick-cook chicken—easily, reliably, traditionally, and terrifically tasty.

SKILLET ITALIANO

Prep **6 MINUTES**   *Cook* **24 MINUTES**

1   tablespoon olive oil

4   boneless, skinless
    chicken breast halves
    (about 1¼ pounds)

1   can (14½ ounces) diced
    tomatoes

1¼ cups water

1   box (6 ounces) rice pilaf

¼   cup chopped fresh basil
    or 1½ teaspoons dried

Kick up the flavor of this chicken in rice even more with a can of flavored tomatoes, perhaps one with garlic and herbs. Substitute homemade stock or canned broth for the water.

LET'S BEGIN Heat the oil in large nonstick skillet over medium-high heat. Cook the chicken for 6 minutes, or until golden brown on both sides.

SIMMER SLOW Stir in the tomatoes with their juice, the water, rice and packet seasonings, and basil. Bring to a boil, then reduce the heat. Cover and simmer for 15 to 18 minutes, until the liquid is absorbed and the chicken juices run clear.

SLICE & SERVE Transfer the chicken to a cutting board and cut crosswise into slices. Serve with rice.

Makes 4 servings

Per serving: 340 calories, 30g protein, 38g carbohydrates, 9g fat, 1g saturated fat, 70mg cholesterol, 960mg sodium

Cooking Basics

3 GREAT 10-MINUTE CHICKEN DINNERS

Looking for something fast and fabulous for dinner? Here are three quick tricks with thin chicken breasts that go from refrigerator to table in just 10 minutes!

For any of the 3 dinners—Place a 5-ounce boneless, skinless chicken breast half (one for each person) between two pieces of plastic wrap or waxed paper.

Pound away on the chicken with the flat side of a cleaver or wooden mallet until it's about ¼-inch thick

making a thin *paillard* cutlet.

Coat the cutlets with a little flour seasoned with salt and pepper. Then, toss into a hot skillet with a little melted butter and cook in a flash over high heat, about

1 minute a side. Finish the *paillards* in one of our three ways from around the world. And supper's ready!

With a German touch—Melt a little sour cream in the skillet and sprinkle with some nutmeg.

With an Italian touch—Drizzle a little Marsala in the skillet and sprinkle with fresh slivered basil.

With an Oriental touch— Spoon over a little teriyaki sauce, straight from a bottle, and sprinkle with crushed roasted peanuts.

SPAGHETTI & MEATBALLS

Prep **10 MINUTES**   *Cook* **35 MINUTES**

Chicken Meatballs
(see recipe)

1   package (16 ounces)
    spaghetti

1   tablespoon olive oil

1   large onion, chopped

1   can (14 ounces) diced
    tomatoes with Italian-
    style herbs

1   can (14 ounces) tomato
    sauce

½   teaspoon salt

¼   teaspoon ground black
    pepper

1   cup grated Parmesan
    cheese (3 ounces)

Make two dinners at once! Just simmer up a double batch of the sauce and meatballs and freeze half. On a busy weekday, heat up the sauce, make some fresh spaghetti and dinner's on the table!

LET'S BEGIN Make the meatballs, then transfer to a plate and keep warm. Meanwhile, cook the spaghetti according to package directions. Drain and keep warm.

MAKE IT SAUCY Using the same skillet, heat the oil over medium heat. Sauté the onion for 3 minutes, or until soft. Stir in the tomatoes with their juice and the tomato sauce. Simmer for 10 minutes.

BUBBLE & STIR Add meatballs, salt, and pepper to the skillet and simmer for 20 minutes. Transfer the spaghetti and meatballs to a platter and serve with the Parmesan.

CHICKEN MEATBALLS

Mix 1 pound ground chicken, 1 large beaten egg, ½ cup grated Parmesan cheese, ½ cup plain dry bread crumbs, 2 minced cloves garlic, 2 teaspoons chopped fresh oregano, and ½ teaspoon salt in a large bowl. Shape into 1-inch balls. Heat 1 tablespoon olive oil in a large nonstick skillet over medium-high heat and brown the meatballs for 5 minutes. Use in above recipe. (To finish cooking meatballs if not using in this recipe, simmer the meatballs in a tomato sauce for about 20 minutes or until cooked through.)

Makes 4 servings

Per serving: 985 calories, 53g protein, 112g carbohydrates, 35 fat, 7g saturated fat, 77mg cholesterol, 2,120mg sodium

RICE-STUFFED POBLANO CHILIES

Prep **15 MINUTES**   *Cook* **35 MINUTES**

1	package (6 ounces) tomato-basil rice mix
2	tablespoons canola oil
1	pound boneless, skinless chicken breast halves, chopped
1	can (14½ ounces) diced tomatoes
1	rib celery, chopped
1	small onion, chopped
4	poblano chilies or small bell peppers, stemmed and seeded
4	ounces shredded Cheddar cheese (1 cup)

Poblano chilies are a medium-hot chile, large, dark green, and shiny. They're often used for stuffing in Mexican and Tex-Mex cuisines, most often in Chiles Rellenos.

LET'S BEGIN Preheat the oven to 350°F. Prepare the rice according to package directions.

SAUTÉ IT QUICK Heat the oil in a large skillet over medium-high heat. Sauté the chicken for 5 minutes, or until brown, then stir in the tomatoes with their juice, the celery, and onion. Cook 5 minutes longer. Stir in the rice.

INTO THE OVEN Spoon the mixture into the peppers, and place in a baking dish. Sprinkle with the cheese. Cover and bake for 25 minutes, or until heated through.

Makes 4 servings

Per serving: 514 calories, 41g protein, 46g carbohydrates, 19g fat, 7g saturated fat, 96mg cholesterol, 1,170mg sodium

---

Microwave in Minutes

MICROWAVE PEPPERS & SUPPER'S READY IN HALF THE TIME!

Steam peppers in the microwave before stuffing them. They'll bake in half the time! The microwave also traps in all their fresh flavor at the same time.

Cut the peppers in half, then seed them. Arrange cut side up on a round microwavable plate and sprinkle with about 2 tablespoons of water. Cover with plastic wrap and leave one corner open so steam can vent and escape.

Steam the peppers on high (in a 600- to 700-watt oven) for 1 minute. Turn over and cook another minute on high. Remove from the oven, wrap in a towel, and let stand for a few minutes. Stuff the peppers, sprinkle with the cheese, cover, and bake in a 350°F oven for about 10 minutes (instead of 25 in regular recipe) or until hot and the cheese bubbles and melts.

GUMBO ON THE BAYOU

Prep **15 MINUTES**   *Cook* **30 MINUTES**

Cooking up a gumbo is cooking like the Cajuns, down on the bayou. The word gumbo comes from the African Congo word for okra (quingombo), *which is traditionally used to thicken the pot.*

1½	**cups long-grain white rice**
2	**tablespoons butter or margarine**
½	**cup chopped green bell pepper**
⅓	**cup chopped onion**
¼	**cup all-purpose flour**
1	**can (15 ounces) whole tomatoes, undrained**
2	**cups diced cooked chicken**
1	**teaspoon dried thyme**
1	**teaspoon salt**
¼	**teaspoon hot pepper sauce**
½	**pound medium shrimp, peeled and deveined**
2	**tablespoons chopped fresh parsley**

LET'S BEGIN Prepare the rice according to package directions and keep warm. Melt the butter in a large Dutch oven over medium-high heat. Sauté the green pepper and onion for 5 minutes, or until tender. Stir in the flour.

SIMMER LOW Add the tomatoes, chicken, thyme, salt, and hot pepper sauce, breaking up the tomatoes with a spoon. Reduce the heat, cover the pot, and simmer for 20 minutes.

STIR & SERVE Add the shrimp and cook for 5 minutes, or until opaque. Toss the rice and parsley together. Place a mound of rice in each large soup bowl and ladle in the gumbo.

Makes 6 servings

Per serving: 380 calories, 26g protein, 46g carbohydrates, 9g fat, 4g saturated fat, 110mg cholesterol, 681mg sodium

Pennsylvania Dutch Chicken Bake

PENNSYLVANIA DUTCH CHICKEN BAKE

Prep **10 MINUTES**   *Cook/Bake* **37 MINUTES**

2	pounds skinless chicken thighs

Salt and ground black pepper

1	large tart red apple
¼	cup canola oil
1	can (16 ounces) sauerkraut, undrained
1	can (15 ounces) whole onions, drained
12	dried apricot halves
½	cup raisins
¼	cup packed brown sugar

Most Pennsylvania Dutch food is home-grown, comforting, and filled with rich flavors. This fast-to-fix dish fits all three.

LET'S BEGIN Preheat the oven to 350°F. Season the chicken with salt and pepper. Core and thinly slice the apple. Heat the oil in a large nonstick skillet over medium-high heat. Sauté the chicken for 6 minutes on each side, or until brown.

INTO THE OVEN Combine the apple and remaining ingredients in a 12x9-inch baking dish. Tuck the thighs into the sauerkraut. Bake for 30 minutes, or until the juices run clear.

Makes 4 servings

Per serving: 463 calories, 28g protein, 48g carbohydrates, 19g fat, 2g saturated fat, 107mg cholesterol, 1,275mg sodium

SuperQuick
ORIENTAL STIR-FRY

Prep **10 MINUTES**   *Cook* **20 MINUTES**

⅔	cup white rice
1	pound boneless, skinless chicken breast halves
1½	tablespoons oil
2	medium carrots, thinly sliced
½	cup onion
1	teaspoon dried basil
1	cup fresh or frozen snow peas
1	tablespoon water
1	medium apple, cored and thinly sliced

Add a dash of flash with a few tablespoons of toasted sesame seeds.

LET'S BEGIN Prepare the rice according to package directions and keep warm. Cut chicken into bite-size chunks.

STIR-FRY Meanwhile, heat 1 tablespoon of the oil in a wok or large nonstick skillet over medium-high heat. Stir-fry the chicken for 5 minutes, or until the juices run clear, and transfer to a bowl. Add the remaining ½ tablespoon oil, the carrots, onion, and basil to the wok and stir-fry for 2 minutes.

TOSS & SERVE Stir in the snow peas and water and stir-fry 2 minutes longer. Remove from the heat and stir in the apple and chicken. Spoon over the hot rice.

Makes 4 servings

Per serving: 365 calories, 30g protein, 33g carbohydrates, 9g fat, 1g saturated fat, 62mg cholesterol, 71mg sodium

TERIYAKI RICE BOWL

Prep **20 MINUTES**   *Marinate* **15 MINUTES**   *Cook* **7 MINUTES**

The word teri *means "gloss" and the word* yaki *means "broiled" in Japanese. Fittingly, teriyaki sauce is a sweet and glossy glaze, wonderful used as a marinade as well as a sauce.*

1⅓   cups long-grain white rice

1½   pounds boneless, skinless chicken breast halves, cut into ½-inch-wide strips

½   cup thick teriyaki sauce

2   tablespoons sugar

2   teaspoons cornstarch

2   tablespoons vegetable oil

3   cups steamed mixed vegetables, such as snow peas and carrots

LET'S BEGIN Cook the rice according to package directions and keep warm. Put the chicken into a resealable plastic bag. Stir the teriyaki sauce and sugar together in a glass measuring cup until the sugar dissolves. Spoon 3 tablespoons of the teriyaki mixture over the chicken. Press out the air and seal the bag. Turn the bag over several times to coat the chicken evenly. Marinate in the refrigerator for 15 minutes. Add enough water to the remaining teriyaki mixture to equal ⅔ cup. Whisk in the cornstarch until blended.

MAKE IT SAUCY Heat the oil in a large skillet over medium-high heat. Sauté the chicken for 5 minutes (discard any sauce in the bag). Add the remaining ⅔ cup sauce and sauté for 1 minute longer, or until sauce thickens and boils.

SERVE IT UP Spoon the rice into large shallow bowls. Top with the chicken and vegetables.

Makes 6 servings

Per serving: 375 calories, 31g protein, 46g carbohydrates, 6g fat, 1g saturated fat, 66mg cholesterol, 900mg sodium

---

Time Savers

4 EASY KITCHEN SHORTCUTS

Save a minute or two (and many more!), day by day, with the most common cooking tasks:

STICK-PROOF SLICING
Before slicing raw boneless chicken breasts into strips, pop it into the freezer a few minutes to firm it up. Then speed up the slicing by spraying your knife with cooking spray before taking a slice.

DAY-AHEAD VEGGIES
Fresh vegetables, such as the snow peas and carrots in this Chicken Teriyaki Rice Bowl, can be cleaned, cut, and blanched in boiling salted water the day before. To heat, sauté a couple of minutes in a little oil until hot.

RICE-ON-HAND
Whenever cooking rice, double the amount and refrigerate the extra. To reheat, place the rice in a strainer over a pot of boiling water and cover. Steam until hot.

PRECOOK PASTA
Take a tip from the restaurant pros: precook pasta ahead until it's slightly underdone. Toss into ice water and cool to room temperature. Drain, toss it with a little olive oil, and refrigerate in zipper-closing bags. Reheat in boiling water in seconds.

SPICED-UP THAI SALAD

Prep **5 MINUTES**   *Cook* **20 MINUTES**

Use jasmine rice for this great Thai-style salad. It's an aromatic rice, which perfumes your entire house as it cooks.

1	cup long-grain white rice
1	package (6 ounces) grilled chicken breast strips, cut into ½-inch pieces
6	cups coleslaw mix
¼	cup chopped fresh cilantro
1	jar (11½ ounces) Thai peanut sauce
¼	cup vegetable oil
¼	cup water
¾	cup coarsely chopped dry-roasted peanuts

LET'S BEGIN Prepare the rice according to package directions. Meanwhile, mix the chicken, coleslaw mix, and cilantro together in a large serving bowl. Add the rice and toss to combine.

TOSS IT Whisk the peanut sauce, oil, and water together in a medium bowl. Drizzle the sauce over the rice mixture and toss to mix well.

SPRINKLE & SERVE Sprinkle with the peanuts.

Makes 6 servings

Per serving: 499 calories, 20g protein, 46g carbohydrates, 27g fat, 4g saturated fat, 24mg cholesterol, 698mg sodium

---

Cook to Cook

HOW CAN I COOK LIKE THEY DO IN THAI RESTAURANTS?

❝*Thai cooking is fast cooking!* This means all the ingredients must be chopped or diced before that first ingredient goes into the pan. Then, keep moving the pan while stirring and tossing constantly as you cook.

Many Thai dishes are stir-fries, so I use a wok. As food cooks, keep pushing it up the sides before adding the next ingredient. If you don't have a wok, grab the biggest skillet you have…if it has sloping sides, that's even better. Keep the food moving and cooking fast!

Thai cooking is more than spicy… salty, sweet, and sour flavors are just as important. And all work with chicken! I use my favorite stir-fry, tossing in whatever I find fresh at the market, just like the chefs do. I keep tasting and adding a little sugar, salt, or sour lime until it tastes just right.

Remember the rice! Many Thai dishes (especially chicken) are meant to be eaten with rice…they call it *gab kao.*❞

CHICKEN & MACADAMIA FRIED RICE

Prep **10 MINUTES**   *Cook* **20 MINUTES**

1	cup basmati rice
2	tablespoons vegetable oil
2	large eggs, beaten
3	cups cubed cooked chicken
1	can (8 ounces) pineapple tidbits, drained
3	scallions, thinly sliced
½	cup salted dry-roasted macadamia nuts, coarsely chopped
2	tablespoons soy sauce or to taste

Ground black pepper

Fried rice is a classic crowd pleaser. If you don't have basmati, use jasmine or any short- or long-grain white rice instead.

LET'S BEGIN Cook rice according to package directions and keep warm. Meanwhile, heat 1 tablespoon of the oil in a wok or large skillet over medium-high heat. Add the eggs and stir-fry for 3 minutes, or until set. Transfer to a small bowl.

STIR-FRY Add the remaining 1 tablespoon oil to the skillet. Add the chicken, pineapple, scallions, nuts, soy sauce, and rice to the wok. Stir-fry for 4 minutes, or until mixed well and heated through.

MIX & SERVE Add the eggs to the wok and season with pepper. Stir-fry for 1 minute longer.

Makes 6 servings

Per serving: 403 calories, 26g protein, 30g carbohydrates, 21g fat, 4g saturated fat, 133mg cholesterol, 455mg sodium

Cooking Basics

3 WAYS TO THAW CHICKEN FAST

THE FASTEST THAW
Use the microwave for the fastest thaw. When thawing chicken breasts with the bones in, place them with thick edges facing the edge of the plate, thin edges inward, and center of dish empty. Cover with waxed paper and follow your manufacturer's directions on thawing. Check for instructions for thawing both whole birds and other pieces.

THE COLD WATER THAW
For a fast thaw, but one that's a little less fast than thawing in the microwave), fill a sink with cold water. Add the wrapped frozen chicken and put a skillet or pot on top to keep it submerged. Allow

about 2 to 3 hours to thaw a 4-pound chicken and 1 hour for chicken parts. Refill the sink with fresh cold water once or twice.

THE EASIEST THAW
To thaw a 4-pound chicken in the refrigerator, put the bird, still in its wrapper, on a plate and refrigerate (just forget it!). Expect it to thaw in about 24 hours for a whole bird, 6 hours for every pound of pieces.

SuperQuick
CHICKEN CACCIATORE
Prep **5 MINUTES**   *Cook* **20 MINUTES**

4   boneless, skinless chicken breast halves (about 1¼ pounds)

1   package (16 ounces) frozen broccoli, cauliflower, and carrots

1   can (14½ ounces) pasta sauce

½   cup drained sliced ripe black olives

¼   cup water

Salt and ground black pepper

¼   cup grated Parmesan cheese

This simplified version of chicken "hunter's style" will have dinner on the table in no time at all. For a classic combination, serve with some precooked polenta from your grocer's refrigerated section.

LET'S BEGIN Cut the chicken crosswise into strips. Spray a large skillet with cooking spray and set over medium heat. Sauté the chicken for 7 to 10 minutes, or until brown.

MAKE IT SAUCY Add the vegetables, pasta sauce, olives, and water to the skillet. Season with salt and pepper. Cover and cook for 10 to 15 minutes, until the vegetables are heated through and chicken juices run clear.

SPRINKLE & SERVE Sprinkle with the cheese.

Makes 4 servings

Per serving: 353 calories, 39g protein, 27g carbohydrates, 9g fat, 3g saturated fat, 86mg cholesterol, 970mg sodium

---

Food Facts

BOOST FLAVOR INSTANTLY WITH OLIVES AROUND THE WORLD

Pick an olive off a tree, take a bite, and you'll discover it's almost inedible. That's the reason olives never come to market right off the trees. They must first be cured— either in oil, water, brine, salt, or lye—and transformed into wonderful flavor-packed tidbits. Every olive starts green, then turns darker as it ripens. The fully ripened black ones turn softer, oilier, and less bitter than their green cousins.

WHAT'S IN A NAME?
Most olives are named for their place of origin, such as tiny black Niçoise from France, brownish-black wrinkled Gaetas from Italy, green Manzanillas from Spain, and almond-shaped, black-purple Kalamatas from Greece.

SAFE HAVEN
Store olives longer by floating a thin layer of olive oil on the surface of the brine. If a white film develops on the surface of the olives, just wipe it off, rinse the olives…and they're ready to go.

THE BIG ROLLOVER
Pit olives easily by rolling over them with a rolling pin, or whacking them with the wide flat side of a chef's knife. This should split the olives and make it easy to remove the pits—in an instant.

WALNUT CHICKEN FOR A CROWD

Prep **10 MINUTES**   *Marinate* **2 HOURS**   *Grill* **15 MINUTES**

½   cup reduced-sodium soy sauce

½   cup dry sherry or chicken broth

⅓   cup vegetable oil

⅓   cup sugar

3   garlic cloves, minced

2   tablespoons grated peeled fresh ginger

10   skinless, boneless chicken breast halves (about 3 pounds)

LEMON-OLIVE SAUCE

½   cup nonfat mayonnaise

½   cup plain nonfat yogurt

3   tablespoons lemon juice

3   tablespoons chopped green or ripe olives

1   garlic clove, minced

Salt and ground black pepper

½   cup California chopped walnuts

Toasting walnuts brings out their flavor. Stir-fry them fast in a dry skillet over medium-high heat, flipping them until they're fragrant.

LET'S BEGIN To make the marinade, whisk the soy sauce, sherry, oil, sugar, garlic, and ginger together in a medium bowl until the sugar dissolves. Reserve ½ cup of the marinade. Put the chicken in one or two resealable plastic bags and pour in the remaining marinade. Press out the air and seal the bag, then turn it over several times to coat the chicken. Marinate in the refrigerator for at least 2 or up to 6 hours.

FIRE UP THE GRILL Preheat the grill or broiler to high. Cook chicken, turning and brushing with the reserved marinade, for 15 minutes, or until the chicken juices run clear.

MAKE IT SAUCY For the sauce, combine mayonnaise, yogurt, lemon juice, olives, and garlic. (Or purée in a food processor.) Season with salt and pepper. Arrange the chicken on a platter, top with the walnuts, and serve with the sauce.

Makes 10 servings

Per serving: 320 calories, 34g protein, 13g carbohydrates, 13g fat, 2g saturated fat, 79mg cholesterol, 735mg sodium

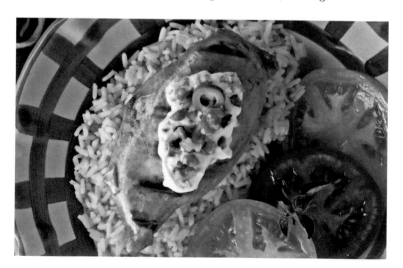

SuperQuick
15-MINUTE TACOS
Prep **5 MINUTES**   *Cook* **10 MINUTES**

Tex-Mex dishes rate some of the highest among melting pot favorites. And here's one you can stir up, simmer up, and shape up in just 15 minutes!

1	tablespoon oil
1	pound boneless, skinless chicken breast halves, cut into strips
2	cups water
1	cup thick 'n' chunky salsa
1	package (1¼ ounces) taco seasoning mix
2	cups uncooked minute rice
10	flour tortillas
2	cups shredded Cheddar cheese (optional)

LET'S BEGIN Heat the oil in a large skillet over medium-high heat. Sauté the chicken for 5 minutes, or until the juices run clear.

BUBBLE & BOIL Add the water, salsa, and seasoning mix and bring to a boil. Stir in the rice and cover. Reduce the heat and simmer for 5 minutes, or until the rice is tender.

ROLL & SERVE Spoon the chicken filling in the center of each tortilla and sprinkle with cheese, if you wish. Fold up sides to enclose filling. Serve 2 tacos to each person.

Makes 5 servings
Per serving: 470 calories, 29g protein, 70g carbohydrates, 7g fat, 2g saturated fat, 55mg cholesterol, 1,180mg sodium

On the Menu

Here's a fast-to-fix supper party that's easy enough to prepare spur-of-moment

Spicy Guacamole with White Corn Chips

15-Minute Tacos

Tomato, Cucumber, & Onion Chopped Salad

Vanilla Ice Cream with Crushed Praline Topping

Sangria

CHICKEN SCHNITZEL WITH LEMON

Prep **15 MINUTES**   *Cook* **6 MINUTES**

4   boneless, skinless
     chicken breast halves
     (about 1¼ pounds)

⅓   cup all-purpose flour

½   teaspoon salt

¼   teaspoon ground black
     pepper

2   large eggs

1   cup plain dry bread
     crumbs

¼   cup vegetable oil

2   tablespoons butter or
     margarine

1   lemon, cut into wedges

Usually made with either veal or pork, these golden chicken paillards are perfect with a squeeze of lemon. Serve noodles and steamed asparagus for an elegant simple meal.

LET'S BEGIN Pound the chicken breasts between plastic wrap until ½-inch thick. Mix the flour, salt, and pepper together on a sheet of waxed paper. Lightly beat the eggs in a shallow dish. Put the bread crumbs on a separate sheet of waxed paper.

DIP & COAT Coat the chicken with the seasoned flour, shaking off the excess, Dip it into the egg, allowing the excess to drip off. Coat the chicken with the bread crumbs and place on a separate sheet of waxed paper.

SAUTÉ IT QUICK Heat the oil with the butter in a large nonstick skillet over medium-high heat. Cook the chicken, turning once, for 6 to 8 minutes, or until deep brown and the juices run clear. Transfer the chicken to a paper towel–lined plate to drain. Serve the schnitzel with the lemon wedges.

Makes 4 servings

Per serving: 517 calories, 41g protein, 31g carbohydrates, 26g fat, 7g saturated fat, 205mg cholesterol, 710mg sodium

EASY CHICKEN STROGANOFF

Prep **10 MINUTES**   *Cook* **20 MINUTES**

8   ounces fresh egg noodles

4   boneless, skinless
       chicken breast halves
       (about 1½ pounds)

2   tablespoons all-purpose
       flour

2   tablespoons butter or
       margarine

1   medium red onion,
       chopped

8   ounces mushrooms,
       quartered

1½   cups chicken broth

2   tablespoons whole-grain
       mustard

½   cup sour cream

3   tablespoons chopped
       fresh parsley

Salt and ground black pepper

The original stroganoff, named after the 19th-century Russian diplomat Count Paul Stroganov, used beef. Thanks to canned broth and fresh egg noodles, our chicken version is ready in mere minutes.

LET'S BEGIN Cook the noodles according to package directions and keep warm. Place the flour on a piece of waxed paper and coat the chicken (reserve any extra flour). Melt the butter in a large nonstick skillet over high heat.

SAUTÉ IT QUICK Cook the chicken, turning once, for 5 minutes, or until brown. Stir in the onion, mushrooms, and any reserved extra flour. Reduce the heat to medium and sauté for 5 minutes, or until the onion is golden brown.

SAUCE IT UP Whisk the broth and mustard together in a small bowl and stir into the skillet. Bring to boil. Reduce the heat and simmer for 5 minutes. Stir in the sour cream and parsley and simmer for 2 more minutes, or until hot (do not boil). Season with salt and pepper and serve over noodles.

Makes 4 servings

Per serving: 403 calories, 37g protein, 30g carbohydrates, 15g fat, 8g saturated fat, 122mg cholesterol, 555mg sodium

---

Food Facts

THE MANY TYPES OF MUSHROOMS

What do dog pecker, chicken of the woods, moocher, pinecone, cloud-ear, ink caps, and man-on-a-horse have in common? Simple...they're all names of mushrooms. Some are cultivated domestically, such as the common white buttons and others are dug up wild from forests, such as the morels, chanterelles, and porcini. Still other exotic and unusual mushrooms are now cultivated and easy-to-find. Try enokis (long, thin, white-stemmed with tiny caps), oysters (smooth and mild-flavored), shiitakes (slightly meaty-tasting and often used in stir-fries), and portobellos (the meaty-tasting ones). Find them all in your local market.

Barbecue Packets, page 110

Fire Up the Grill!

Use the grill or the broiler for quick-cooking chicken any day, any time. Here, you'll find everyone's favorite of barbecued chicken in many ways: mopped with Carolina sauce, skewered into kabobs, rubbed with hot mustards, spiced with fresh ginger, grilled with fresh vegetables, and flavored ahead with fresh herb marinades. Learn the secrets of grilling chicken so it always comes off the grill, golden brown and glazed on the outside, juicy and tender on the inside. Discover how your outdoor grill or your indoor broiler can help you create more great-tasting ways to cook and serve chicken—effortlessly, easily, and simply delicious—in a matter of minutes.

EASY BARBECUE KABOBS

Prep **20 MINUTES**   *Grill* **10 MINUTES**

1   can (20 ounces)
    pineapple chunks,
    drained, 2 tablespoons
    juice reserved

⅓   cup barbecue sauce

1   pound boneless, skinless
    chicken breast halves,
    cut into 1-inch chunks

1   red or green bell pepper,
    cut into 1-inch pieces

1   medium zucchini, cut
    into ½-inch-thick slices

To grill these kabobs faster in one-third less time, use 8 skewers instead of 4. Since the chicken and vegetables are threaded further apart, heat circulates more quickly and food cooks faster.

LET'S BEGIN Soak 4 wooden skewers in hot water. Meanwhile, stir the reserved pineapple juice and barbecue sauce together in a small bowl.

FIRE UP THE GRILL Preheat the grill or broiler. Thread the pineapple chunks, chicken, bell pepper, and zucchini onto the skewers.

MAKE IT SAUCY Grill (or broil) the kabobs, turning and brushing occasionally with the pineapple barbecue sauce, for 10 to 15 minutes, or just until the chicken juices run clear.

Makes 4 servings

Per serving: 281 calories, 37g protein, 23g carbohydrates, 5g fat, 1g saturated fat, 96mg cholesterol, 255mg sodium

North Carolina Barbeque

Prep **15 MINUTES**   *Marinate* **1 HOUR**   *Grill* **10 MINUTES**

2	pounds boneless, skinless chicken breast halves or thighs
¾	cup light brown sugar
¾	cup yellow mustard
½	cup cider vinegar
¼	cup hot pepper sauce
2	tablespoons vegetable oil
2	tablespoons Worcestershire sauce
½	teaspoon salt
¼	teaspoon ground pepper

You won't find any tomato in the barbecue pits in eastern North Carolina. But you will discover this spicy, vinegary, richly flavored sauce. It's often served with coleslaw, spiced with a little turmeric.

LET'S BEGIN Put the chicken into a resealable plastic bag. Stir ½ cup of the brown sugar, the mustard, vinegar, pepper sauce, oil, Worcestershire, salt, and pepper together in a 4-cup glass measuring cup. Pour 1 cup of the mustard mixture over the chicken. Press out the air and seal the bag. Marinate in the refrigerator for at least 1 hour or up to overnight.

MAKE IT SAUCY Bring the remaining mustard mixture and the sugar to a boil in a small saucepan. Reduce the heat and simmer for 5 minutes, or until mixture thickens slightly.

FIRE UP THE GRILL Preheat the grill and oil the grill rack. Grill the chicken, turning once, for 10 to 15 minutes, or until the juices run clear. Serve with the reserved sauce.

Makes 8 servings
Per serving: 226 calories, 27g protein, 17g carbohydrates, 6g fat, 1g saturated fat, 66mg cholesterol, 565mg sodium

Microwave in Minutes

CUT GRILLING TIME 50 PERCENT

Let your microwave help save you grilling time. Here's how: Arrange the chicken pieces on a microwavable plate with the meatier, thicker parts pointing outward to the edge. Cover with waxed paper. Microwave on high for 1 minute, then turn over and cook 1 minute more, or just until the chicken feels semifirm. Transfer to the grill to finish cooking (it'll take about half the time as the recipe calls for).

THAI SKEWERS

Prep **20 MINUTES**   *Marinate* **6 HOURS**   *Grill* **6 MINUTES**

¼ cup smooth peanut butter

2 tablespoons finely chopped onion

2 tablespoons lemon juice

1½ teaspoons soy sauce

1 garlic clove, minced

1 teaspoon hot pepper sauce

2 tablespoons chopped fresh parsley

1 pound boneless, skinless chicken breast halves

Throw together the chicken and marinade in the morning and refrigerate. In the evening, all it needs is a quick grill.

LET'S BEGIN Stir together all of the ingredients except the chicken in a medium bowl.

COAT & CHILL Cut the chicken into 1-inch-wide strips, and add to the bowl. Toss to coat. Cover and refrigerate for 6 hours or up to overnight. Meanwhile, soak 4 wooden skewers in hot water for about 30 minutes.

FIRE UP THE GRILL Preheat the grill or broiler to medium. Thread chicken onto the skewers. Cook the chicken, turning frequently, for 6 minutes, or until the juices run clear.

Makes 4 servings

Per serving: 227 calories, 31g protein, 5g carbohydrates, 10g fat, 2g saturated fat, 66mg cholesterol, 286mg sodium

---

Cook to Cook

HOW CAN I MAKE SURE EVERYTHING ON THE GRILL GETS DONE AT THE SAME TIME?

" *Wait until the fire's ready to put on the food.* This avoids overcooking the food at the very beginning. And watch the flames carefully. After they've died down, wait until the coals turn a white ashen color. Even out the heat by spreading out the coals. Now, put on the food (be sure it's all at room temperature).

Put the food on in an orderly pattern, so you'll always know what's been cooking the longest. When cooking chicken, arrange the meatier pieces in the center, the thinner ones toward the edge.

Stay in control of the fire, and you'll be in control of how fast or slow foods are cooking. Keep a spray bottle of water around to snuff out any flare-ups. Use the cover, if your grill has one, or place an upside-down aluminum pan over the food if there's not a cover.

Use tongs, not a fork to turn the foods. This keeps in the juices and prevents fat from dripping onto the fire. Fat drizzling onto the fire not only causes flare-ups but also can burn food fast.

Keep foods moving from the hotter center of the grill to the cooler sides. Turn the cooked parts toward the sides of grill. "

GRILLED CHICKEN SATAYS

Prep **25 MINUTES**   *Marinate* **30 MINUTES**   *Grill* **5 MINUTES**

1   pound boneless, skinless
     chicken breast halves,
     cut lengthwise into
     1-inch-wide strips

Peanut Sauce (see recipe)

Chopped fresh cilantro

Cucumber slices

Satays come from our Indonesian friends. Make them the authentic way by seasoning up chicken with a peanut sauce, then gilling them in just 5 minutes until they sizzle.

LET'S BEGIN   Soak 8 (6-inch) wooden skewers in hot water. Thread the chicken onto the skewers. Prepare the sauce.

MAKE IT SAUCY   Put the skewers into a large, shallow baking dish and pour ⅔ cup of the peanut sauce over them, turning to coat. Reserve the remaining peanut sauce. Cover and refrigerate for at least 30 minutes or up to several hours.

FIRE UP THE GRILL   Oil the grill rack and preheat the grill to high. Grill the chicken, turning once, for 5 to 8 minutes, or until the juices run clear. Transfer to a platter and sprinkle with the cilantro. Serve with the cucumber slices and the reserved sauce.

PEANUT SAUCE

Combine ⅓ cup peanut butter, ⅓ cup Dijon mustard, ⅓ cup orange juice, 1 tablespoon chopped peeled fresh ginger, 1 tablespoon honey, 1 tablespoon hot pepper sauce, 1 tablespoon teriyaki baste-and-glaze sauce, and 2 minced garlic cloves in a small bowl.

> *Makes 8 appetizer servings*
> *Per serving: 165 calories, 17g protein, 9g carbohydrates, 7g fat, 1g saturated fat, 33mg cholesterol, 207mg sodium*

BBQ & Grilled Vegetables
Prep **10 minutes**   *Grill* **14 minutes**

¾   cup barbecue sauce

4   boneless, skinless
     chicken breast halves
     (about 1¼ pounds)

¼   cup zesty Italian
     dressing

1   medium zucchini, cut
     lengthwise in half

1   yellow squash, cut
     lengthwise in half

1   large green bell pepper,
     cut lengthwise into
     quarters

1   large red bell pepper,
     cut lengthwise into
     quarters

Here's chicken BBQ and veggies, plain American style with all the original flavors of tomato, spice, and smoke. For variety, also try: parboiled sweet-potato slices, parboiled whole carrots, sliced eggplant, thick tomato slices, thick white onion slices.

LET'S BEGIN Slather some of the barbecue sauce on the chicken with a spoon. With a brush spread some of the dressing over the vegetables.

FIRE UP THE GRILL Oil the grill rack. Preheat grill to high. Grill chicken, covered, for 4 minutes. Add vegetables.

MAKE IT SAUCY Cook, turning once, for 10 minutes, or until chicken juices run clear and vegetables are tender. Brush chicken often with sauce and vegetables with dressing.

Makes 4 servings

Per serving: 310 calories, 32g protein, 22g carbohydrates, 9g fat, 2g saturated fat, 85mg cholesterol, 950mg sodium

Surf 'n' Turf Grill

Prep **15 MINUTES**   *Marinate* **2 HOURS**   *Grill* **6 MINUTES**

SPICY MARINADE

⅔	cup white wine vinegar
½	cup soy sauce
2	tablespoons olive oil
2	tablespoons dark or light sesame oil
2	scallions, sliced
2	tablespoons minced peeled fresh ginger
2	large garlic cloves, minced
2	teaspoons hot pepper sauce
1	pound medium shrimp, peeled and deveined, tails left on
4	boneless, skinless chicken breast halves (about 1¼ pounds)

Here's a true fix-and-forget grill that takes only minutes to whisk up and just 6 minutes to grill.

LET'S BEGIN Soak 4 wooden skewers in hot water. Meanwhile, whisk all marinade ingredients in a small bowl. Set aside ⅓ cup. Pour remaining marinade into a 13x9-inch shallow baking dish. Thread the shrimp onto the skewers and place them with the chicken in the baking dish, turning to coat well.

LET IT CHILL Cover and refrigerate for at least 2 or up to 24 hours, turning the skewers and chicken several times.

FIRE UP THE GRILL Preheat the grill to medium. Grill the chicken for 3 minutes. Place the shrimp skewers on the grill and discard any marinade remaining in the dish. Grill the shrimp and chicken, turning once and brushing with the reserved marinade, for 3 minutes, or until the shrimp are opaque throughout and the chicken juices run clear.

Makes 4 servings

Per serving: 437 calories, 58g protein, 6g carbohydrates, 17g fat, 3g saturated fat, 255mg cholesterol, 2,338mg sodium

---

Cook to Cook

DOES THAT BEER CAN & CHICKEN TRICK REALLY WORK?

"Yes, it does! *Sometimes I use a can of cola,* sometimes beer, other times root beer. Here's all you do: take a can of soda or beer, pour out (or drink!) about a ½ cup of it, then punch a couple of extra holes in the top of the can. Now take about a 3- to 4-pound chicken and rub it with some spices if you like (the hotter the better!). *Stand the bird up over the half-full can* (with the liquid still inside) and place on the grill, away from the hottest coals. The bird will look a little like a teepee, as it rests on the can and its drumsticks. Now just cover the grill and walk away for about an hour. You might check it a couple of times and twist the bird around. As the bird cooks, the soda gets hot, bubbles up, and steams the bird. *The chicken cooks faster than usual* and comes out juicy, moist, and tasting great!"

SuperQuick
BARBECUE PACKETS
Prep **10 MINUTES**   _Grill_ **12 MINUTES**

4   boneless, skinless chicken breast halves (1¼ to 1½ pounds)

4   sheets (12x18 inches) heavy-duty aluminum foil

1   cup barbecue sauce

1   cup corn kernels (fresh or canned and drained)

½   cup chopped green bell pepper

Here's dinner in minutes without fuss, muss, or cleanup. Just fold up the foil packets, put on the grill, and supper cooks itself in minutes.

LET'S BEGIN Place a chicken breast in center of each piece of foil. Spoon over ¼ cup sauce. Top with corn and bell pepper. Close the foil packets, bringing up the sides. Double-fold the top and ends, leaving room for heat to circulate.

FIRE UP THE GRILL Preheat the grill to medium-hot and place packets on rack. Cook, covered, 12 to 15 minutes, or until chicken juices run clear and the vegetables are tender.

> _Makes 4 servings_
>
> _Per serving: 252 calories, 35g protein, 19g carbohydrates, 3g fat, 1g saturated fat, 82mg cholesterol, 700mg sodium_

GINGER-GLAZED CUTLETS
Prep **15 MINUTES**   _Marinate_ **4 HOURS**   _Grill_ **6 MINUTES**

6   skinless, boneless chicken breast halves (about 2 pounds)

3   cups 100% Niagara white grape juice

¼   cup fresh lemon juice

2   tablespoons grated peeled fresh ginger

2   garlic cloves, minced

1½   teaspoons salt

¼   teaspoon ground pepper

5   tablespoons unsalted butter, cut into pieces

Mix up this marinade from white grape juice in minutes, then let it chill "on its own." Turn extra marinade into a buttery, syrupy sauce.

LET'S BEGIN Place chicken in a large shallow baking dish. Combine all remaining ingredients except butter in a glass measure. Reserve 1 cup of marinade; pour remainder over chicken, and cover. Refrigerate 4 hours, turning occasionally.

FIRE UP THE GRILL Preheat the grill to medium-high. Transfer chicken to grill rack, discarding any extra marinade remaining in the dish. Grill chicken until juices run clear.

SAUCE & SERVE Cook reserved marinade until syrupy. Remove from heat and whisk in butter. Pour over chicken.

> _Makes 6 servings_
>
> _Per serving: 338 calories, 36g protein, 20g carbohydrates, 12g fat, 7g saturated fat, 115mg cholesterol, 685mg sodium_

CHICKEN WITH GRAPE SALSA

Prep **15 MINUTES**   *Grill* **12 MINUTES**

Looking for a fresh new twist on salsa? This is it! Juicy grapes and crispy cucumbers form the perfect complement for tender, fast-grilled chicken—all with little effort from you.

8	boneless chicken thighs (about 2 pounds)
½	cup honey mustard
1	medium cucumber, peeled, seeded, and chopped
2	cups red and/or green seedless grapes, halved
1	teaspoon grated lime zest (optional)
¼	cup lime juice
2	tablespoons olive oil
¼	teaspoon salt
¼	teaspoon ground black pepper

LET'S BEGIN Preheat the gill to medium. Place the chicken between plastic wrap and pound until ½ inch thick. Brush the mustard on both sides of the thighs.

MAKE IT SAUCY To make the salsa, stir all of the remaining ingredients together in a serving bowl.

FIRE UP THE GRILL Grill the chicken, turning once, for 12 minutes, or until the juices run clear. Serve the chicken along with the salsa.

Makes 4 servings
Per serving: 540 calories, 32g protein, 24g carbohydrates, 35g fat, 9g saturated fat, 150mg cholesterol, 525mg sodium

---

Food Facts

THE VERY BEST AMERICAN BBQ

Every good American barbecue begins with cooking foods in pits with lots of smoke. Here, the similarities stop. The rubs, sauce, and fire vary from region to region.

NORTH CAROLINIAN PIG PICKIN'S

Deep in the back country of North Carolina, you'll find those popular pig pickin's (slow-smoking whole hogs). Sink your teeth into their famous pulled pork, loaded with a peppery vinegar sauce.

RUB THOSE TENNESSEE BACKS

Come down south to Memphis, the home of the "dry rubs." Here, baby backs are coated with a dry seasoning rub, then slowly smoked.

KANSAS CITY DRY-RUB RIBS

Look for more dry-rubbing and smoking in Kansas City. But here, ribs are also slathered with a thick tomato-ey sauce.

DOWN ON A TEXAS RANCH

Stop by a Texas ranch for some and enjoy beef brisket, chicken, and ribs—all mopped with a spicy, hickory-smoked tomato-ey sauce for that finger-lickin' great flavor.

Outdoor Grill with Fresh Herbs

Prep **15 MINUTES** *Roast* **30 MINUTES**

Marinate **15 MINUTES** *Grill* **10 MINUTES**

Roasting shallots and garlic turns them sweet and mild. Whirl them up with bacon and herbs for a marinade that doubles as a salsa.

3	slices bacon, halved crosswise
6	shallots, peeled
6	garlic cloves, peeled
¾	cup extra-virgin olive oil
6	tablespoons balsamic vinegar

Juice of 1 large lemon

1	tablespoon each: chopped fresh basil, chives, rosemary, and sage
8	chicken breast halves (about 4 pounds), bones removed and skin left on

LET'S BEGIN Preheat the oven to 350°F. Combine the bacon, shallots, garlic, and 6 tablespoons of the oil in a large ovenproof skillet. Roast for 30 minutes, or until brown, transferring the bacon to paper towels to drain when it is cooked crisp.

SEASON & SPICE Pulse bacon, shallot mixture, remaining oil, and all remaining ingredients except chicken in a food processor until finely chopped. Put the chicken in a shallow baking dish and smear with half of the bacon mixture (chill other half). Cover dish. Refrigerate for 15 minutes or overnight.

FIRE UP THE GRILL Preheat the grill. Grill the chicken, turning, for 10 minutes, or until the juices run clear. Heat the reserved bacon mixture and serve with the chicken.

Makes 8 servings

Per serving: 425 calories, 25g protein, 9g carbohydrates, 33g fat, 6g saturated fat, 75mg cholesterol, 131mg sodium

---

Cooking Basics

GRILL CHICKEN FAST & JUICY!

Grilling is by nature one of the best types of fast cooking—especially since food cooks directly over hot live flames (at least 500°F). This hot heat caramelizes the sugars, bringing out incredible flavors in the chicken. So, light the fire, wait until the flames die down, and put on the chicken.

CONTROL CHARCOAL
To make the fire hotter and cook faster, open the grill vents, push coals together, and tap the coals to loosen any ash. To slow down the fire, partially close the vents.

AVOID STICKUPS
Keep food from sticking by first heating the rack over the fire. Wearing mitts, remove rack and coat with cooking spray or rub with oil. Return rack to grill and start grilling. Baste frequently!

BBQ THE WHOLE BIRD
Butterfly a 3- to 4-pound bird (see page 118). Marinate if you wish and grill over medium coals in half the time, about 25 minutes per side, or until the juices run clean.

ROSEMARY CHICKEN

Prep **15 MINUTES**   *Marinate* **30 MINUTES**   *Grill* **20 MINUTES**

4	boneless skinless chicken breast halves (about 1¼ pounds)
¼	cup yellow mustard
¼	cup frozen orange juice concentrate
2	tablespoons cider vinegar
2	teaspoons dried rosemary, crushed
4	slices thick-cut bacon

Fresh rosemary gives this quick grill an even greater burst of flavor. Use 1 tablespoon snipped fresh leaves for the dried. Put an extra rosemary sprig under the bacon next to the chicken.

LET'S BEGIN Soak four wooden picks in hot water. Put the chicken into a resealable plastic bag. Combine the mustard, orange juice concentrate, vinegar, and rosemary in a glass measuring cup. Set aside ¼ cup of the marinade. Pour the remaining marinade over the chicken. Press out the excess air and seal the bag. Marinate in the refrigerator for 30 minutes.

FIX IT FAST Wrap 1 strip of bacon crosswise around each piece of chicken. Secure with the wooden picks.

FIRE UP THE GRILL Preheat the grill to medium. Grill the chicken, turning and basting often with the reserved marinade, for 20 to 25 minutes, until the juices run clear. Remove the wooden picks before serving.

Makes 4 servings
Per serving: 257 calories, 38g protein, 9g carbohydrates, 7g fat, 2g saturated fat, 92mg cholesterol, 511mg sodium

Time Savers

FIX 2 DINNERS AT ONCE

When marinating chicken, double the marinade, the chicken, and the dinners—but not the time. Freeze a fourth of the marinade in a resealable bag. Marinate all the chicken in the remaining marinade. Cook half the chicken now. Freeze the rest in a clean bag for dinner #2. If you don't have time to whip up a marinade, pick up one. On chicken, try: Caribbean Rum & Lime, Southern Mesquite, Thai Coconut, Island Jerk.

GRILLED LEMON CHICKEN DIJON

Prep **5 MINUTES**   *Marinate* **1 HOUR**   *Grill* **15 MINUTES**

⅓ cup white cooking wine with lemon

⅓ cup olive oil

2 tablespoons Dijon mustard (coarse-grain country-style preferred)

1 teaspoon dried thyme

4 boneless, skinless chicken breast halves (about 1¼ pounds)

Refrigerate chicken in this Dijon marinade in the morning, then grill in minutes in the evening.

LET'S BEGIN Combine the wine, oil, mustard, and thyme in a shallow baking dish. Refrigerate ¼ cup. Add chicken to dish, turning to coat. Cover and refrigerate 1 hour.

FIRE UP THE GRILL Preheat the grill to medium. Remove the chicken and discard any marinade left in dish. Grill chicken, turning once and basting with the reserved marinade, for 15 to 20 minutes, or until the juices run clear.

Makes 4 servings

Per serving: 340 calories, 33g protein, 1g carbohydrate, 20g fat, 3g saturated fat, 82mg cholesterol, 136mg sodium

WEST COAST BARBECUED CHICKEN

Prep **10 MINUTES**   *Marinate* **15 MINUTES**   *Grill* **25 MINUTES**

3 pounds chicken pieces

1 teaspoon salt (optional)

½ teaspoon ground black pepper (optional)

½ cup honey

¼ cup lemon juice or dry white wine

¼ cup soy sauce

1 teaspoon grated orange zest

1 small garlic clove, minced

Barbecue chicken the way they do along the Pacific West Coast. Whip up this fast sweet-and-sour citrus sauce in an instant.

LET'S BEGIN Season chicken with salt and pepper if you wish. Put in a shallow baking dish. Make marinade by whisking all remaining ingredients together. Refrigerate ⅓ cup.

COAT & CHILL Pour the remaining marinade over the chicken, turning to coat. Cover and refrigerate for at least 15 minutes or up to overnight.

FIRE UP THE GRILL Preheat the grill. Cook the chicken, turning it, for 25 minutes, or until juices run clear. Baste the last 10 minutes with the reserved marinade.

Makes 4 servings

Per serving: 450 calories, 28g protein, 38g carbohydrates, 21g fat, 6g saturated fat, 106mg cholesterol, 1,130mg sodium

Grilled Lemon Chicken Dijon

Sweet & Tart Chicken Roast, page 121

Weekend Fare

On those weekends when there's a little more time to spend at home, you can afford to enjoy dishes that need a few extra minutes once they're in the oven. They're still a part of quick-cooking, especially because they help save you cooking time during the week. Roast up a bird one Sunday and quick-mix up soups, sandwiches, and salads from leftovers during the week. Cherry-glaze a chicken, bake up a potpie. Invite friends over for a special chicken taco dish or fry up some chicken for a picnic. Or simply fry up some pecan-crusted chicken for the family. Whichever you choose, you'll find our weekend recipes serve up great taste, fun times, and good eating all week long.

EASY SUNDAY DINNER

Prep **15 MINUTES**   *Roast* **2½ HOURS**

1   chicken (5 to 7 pounds), giblets and neck removed

1   tablespoon olive or vegetable oil

1   package (20 ounces) frozen Parmesan-herb flavored vegetables with seasoning packet (potatoes, broccoli, cauliflower, and carrots)

It's Sunday—time for roast chicken for the whole family. Skip chopping time by using a package of seasoned veggies.

LET'S BEGIN   Preheat the oven to 350°F. Rinse the chicken and pat dry. Rub the skin with oil and season the chicken inside and out with 1 tablespoon of the seasonings from the packet. Place the chicken in a roasting pan.

INTO THE OVEN   Roast the chicken for 2 hours. Scatter the vegetables around the chicken. Sprinkle with the remaining seasonings. Roast 30 minutes longer, or until an instant-read thermometer (inserted in the thigh, not touching the bone) reaches 180°F and the juices run clear. Let the bird rest for 10 minutes to set the juices. Transfer to a platter and surround with the vegetables.

Makes 6 servings

Per serving: 677 calories, 50g protein, 8g carbohydrates, 48g fat, 14g saturated fat, 203mg cholesterol, 575mg sodium

Cooking Basics

ROAST YOUR CHICKEN IN HALF THE TIME

COOK YOUR CHICKEN IN HALF THE TIME

Roasting time varies with the size of the bird, and whether it's stuffed or boned. An unstuffed 5-pound bird is ready to eat about a half-hour sooner than a stuffed one. If you butterfly and flatten out the bird, you cut the roasting time by 50%!

REMOVE THE BREASTBONE

Place the whole bird, breast side up, on a cutting board. Using

poultry or kitchen shears, cut down through the ribs along each side of the backbone, "freeing" it from the ribs. Lift out the backbone.

SPATCHCOCK THE BIRD

Press the palm of your hand against the breastbone and push hard to flatten out the bird. Transfer to a roasting pan and roast. You'll find the bird will be ready in about half the usual time.

DEVILISH CHICKEN

Prep **10 MINUTES**   *Bake* **1 HOUR**

3½   pounds chicken pieces

4   ears corn, husked and silks removed

6   tablespoons butter, melted

2   tablespoons Dijon mustard

2   tablespoons cider vinegar

1   teaspoon dried thyme

½   teaspoon salt

¼   teaspoon ground red pepper

¼   cup plain dry bread crumbs

"Deviled" or "devilish" usually means the dish includes mustard, vinegar, and bread crumbs. Add these to chicken; dinner bakes itself.

LET'S BEGIN Preheat oven to 400°F. Put chicken in a single layer in a large baking dish, and corn in another baking dish.

FIX IT QUICK Stir all remaining ingredients except bread crumbs in a cup. Brush first on corn, then all over chicken. Sprinkle bread crumbs over chicken and cover corn with foil.

INTO THE OVEN Bake for 1 hour, or until the chicken is crispy and the juices run clear and the corn is tender.

Makes 4 servings
Per serving: 763 calories, 42g protein, 20g carbohydrates, 56g fat, 22g saturated fat, 215mg cholesterol, 737mg sodium

CRISP & CRUNCHY OVEN-FRY

Prep **15 MINUTES**   *Bake* **45 MINUTES**

1   chicken (about 3 pounds), cut up or chicken pieces

½   cup mayonnaise

1   tablespoon hot pepper sauce

½   teaspoon onion powder

4   cups corn flakes cereal, crushed into coarse crumbs

¼   cup finely chopped fresh parsley (optional)

If you're feeding a crowd of kids, oven-fry just drumsticks. Double the recipe for a dozen kids—and watch the legs fly off the platter.

LET'S BEGIN Preheat the oven to 375°F. Remove the skin from all but the chicken wings. Mix the mayonnaise, hot pepper sauce, and onion powder together in a small bowl.

DIP & COAT Place the cereal and parsley, if you like, in a large resealable plastic bag. Brush the chicken generously with the mayonnaise mixture. Drop 1 piece of chicken at a time into the crumbs in the bag and shake the bag to coat evenly.

BAKE Bake the chicken, skin side up, in an ungreased baking pan for 45 minutes, or until the juices run clear.

Makes 6 servings
Per serving: 330 calories, 25g protein, 17g carbohydrates, 29g fat, 3g saturated fat, 87mg cholesterol, 340mg sodium

Sweet & Tart Chicken Roast

Prep **20 MINUTES**   *Roast* **1 ¼ HOURS**

1   whole chicken, 3½ to 4 pounds (neck and giblets removed)

½   teaspoon salt

¼   teaspoon ground black pepper

Ground red pepper

1   large lemon, zest grated and reserved

½   cup chicken broth

1   cup fresh cranberries

½   cup kumquats, halved, or chopped tangerine

1   teaspoon prepared horseradish

3   tablespoons maple syrup

2   tablespoons butter

This recipe uses a small bird, so roast chicken is ready in about an hour.

LET'S BEGIN   Preheat the oven to 450° F. Rinse the chicken. Mix the salt and black and red pepper together and sprinkle over the chicken. Place the chicken in a roasting pan, tucking the wings underneath. Cut the lemon in half, squeeze the juice over chicken, and place lemon halves in the chicken cavity.

EASY ROAST   Roast the chicken for 15 minutes. Reduce the heat to 350°F and roast 50 minutes longer, or until an instant-read thermometer (inserted in the thigh, not touching the bone) reaches 180°F and the juices run clear. Transfer the chicken to a cutting board and cover with foil.

SAUCE & SERVE   Pour off the fat from the pan drippings and stir in the broth, lemon zest, and all remaining ingredients except the butter. Bring to a simmer over medium heat and cook for 10 minutes, or until cranberries pop. Reduce heat and stir in the butter until melted. Serve with the chicken.

Makes 4 servings
Per serving: 584 calories, 37g protein, 17g carbohydrates, 40g fat, 13g saturated fat, 172mg cholesterol, 609mg sodium

Devilish Chicken

LEMON-HERB ROAST CHICKEN

Prep **15 MINUTES**   *Marinate* **1 HOUR**   *Roast* **55 MINUTES**

⅓   cup lemon juice
     (about 2 large lemons)

¼   cup dry vermouth,
     dry white wine,
     or chicken broth

¼   cup olive oil

2   teaspoons chopped
     fresh rosemary or
     ½ teaspoon dried

2   teaspoons chopped
     fresh thyme or
     ½ teaspoon dried

1   garlic clove, minced

1   chicken (about 3 pounds)

Lemon, rosemary, and thyme turns this roast chicken into a fabulous supper. It roasts in less than an hour.

LET'S BEGIN Whisk all of the ingredients together except the chicken in a shallow baking dish. Transfer ⅓ cup of the marinade to a covered container and refrigerate. Place the chicken in the baking dish and turn to coat. Cover and refrigerate for 1 to 2 hours, turning the chicken several times.

INTO THE PAN Preheat the oven to 375°F. Transfer the chicken to a rack in a roasting pan. Place it breast side up and tuck the wing tips under the bird. Discard any marinade in the dish. Brush the bird with the reserved marinade.

INTO THE OVEN Roast the chicken for 55 minutes, or until an instant-read thermometer (inserted in the thigh, not touching the bone) registers 180°F and the juices run clear, basting with the marinade. For easier carving, let chicken stand for 10 minutes.

Makes 4 servings

Per serving: 671 calories, 42g protein, 2g carbohydrates, 52g fat, 13g saturated fat, 179mg cholesterol, 168mg sodium

Microwave in Minutes

USE YOUR MICROWAVE TO HELP ROAST A CHICKEN IN HALF THE TIME!

By using the microwave to jump-start the cooking of a whole chicken, you can serve a delicious roasted bird, right out of the oven, in half the time. Here's how...

Spatchcock the bird (page 118) and place the bird, breast side down, on a microwavable plate. Cover loosely with plastic wrap and vent a corner. Microwave on High for 20 minutes, or just until the juices are almost running clear. Be sure to turn over and rotate the bird at least once during microwaving.

Transfer the bird to a rack in a roasting pan and cook in a 375°F oven for about 20 minutes, or until the bird is golden brown on the outside and an instant thermometer registers 175°F. Let the bird rest for 10 minutes before carving.

CHERRY-GLAZED CHICKEN

Prep **10 MINUTES**   *Cook/Bake* **55 MINUTES**

1   cut-up chicken (about 3 pounds) or 6 chicken breast halves

½   cup milk

½   cup all-purpose flour

1   teaspoon dried thyme

Salt and ground black pepper

2   tablespoons vegetable oil

CHERRY SAUCE

1   can (16 ounces) pitted tart cherries, drained, ½ cup juice reserved

¼   cup packed brown sugar

¼   cup granulated sugar

1   teaspoon yellow mustard

Buy tart or sour pie cherries in a can for this chicken as regular sweet cherries will be too sweet. Or use 2 cups frozen unsweetened pitted tart cherries and ½ cup of cherry juice in place of can.

LET'S BEGIN Preheat the oven to 350°F. Rinse the chicken inside and out with cold running water and pat dry with paper towels. Pour the milk into a shallow dish. Mix the flour, thyme, salt, and pepper together on a sheet of waxed paper. Dip each piece of chicken into the milk, then coat with the seasoned flour, shaking off the excess. Heat the oil in a large nonstick skillet over medium-high heat. Cook the chicken for 5 minutes on each side, or until brown. Transfer the chicken as it browns to a 13x9-inch baking dish. Cover with foil and bake for 30 minutes.

MAKE IT SAUCY Meanwhile to make the cherry sauce, combine the reserved cherry juice and both sugars in a small saucepan and bring to a boil over medium heat. Stir in the mustard and cook 5 minutes longer, or until the sauce thickens slightly. Stir in the cherries. (The sauce will continue to thicken once it bakes.)

KEEP BAKING After the chicken has baked for 30 minutes, uncover it, and spoon the hot cherry sauce over. Bake, uncovered, for 15 minutes longer, or until the chicken is tender and the juices run clear.

Makes 6 servings
Per serving: 557 calories, 30g protein, 38g carbohydrates, 31g fat, 8g saturated fat, 122mg cholesterol, 187mg sodium

MANDARIN ORANGE CHICKEN

Prep **5 MINUTES**   *Bake* **35 MINUTES**

⅓   cup dry white wine or chicken broth

⅓   cup frozen orange juice concentrate, thawed

¼   cup sweet orange marmalade

½   teaspoon ground ginger

4   boneless chicken breast halves (about 1¼ pounds)

1   can (11 ounces) mandarin orange segments, drained

½   cup seedless green grapes, halved

Tangerines, clementines, zipper-skin oranges, and kid-glove oranges all qualify as mandarin oranges. They're all sweet and highly perfumed, with skins that slip off fast.

LET'S BEGIN Preheat the oven to 350°F.

TOSS IT Stir the wine, orange juice concentrate, marmalade, and ginger together in a 13x9-inch baking dish. Add the chicken, turning to coat.

INTO THE OVEN Bake the chicken, basting occasionally with the pan juices, for 35 minutes, or until the juices run clear. Add oranges and grapes to the baking dish during the last 5 minutes of cooking.

Makes 4 servings
Per serving: 406 calories, 31g protein, 39g carbohydrates, 13g fat, 4g saturated fat, 91mg cholesterol, 107mg sodium

Cherry-glazed Chicken

PECAN-CRUSTED CHICKEN WITH SWEET-POTATO CHUTNEY

Prep **15 MINUTES**   *Cook* **30 MINUTES**

1   cup all-purpose flour

¾   teaspoon salt

½   teaspoon ground black pepper

3   large eggs

½   cup milk

2   cups coarsely ground toasted pecans

6   boneless, skinless chicken breast halves (2 pounds)

½   cup canola oil

Sweet-Potato Chutney (see recipe)

Fresh mint sprigs

Lemon slices

Red jalapeño peppers

From the heart of pecan country in Texas comes this recipe. Toast the pecans first for a few minutes in a hot skillet. Then grind them finely in a food processor.

LET'S BEGIN Make the Sweet-Potato Chutney. While the chutney cooks, mix the flour, salt, and pepper together on a piece of waxed paper. Whisk the eggs and milk together in a small bowl. Spread the pecans on a shallow plate.

DIP & COAT Coat the chicken in the seasoned flour, shaking off the excess. Dip the chicken into the egg mixture, then coat with the pecans.

SAUTÉ IT QUICK Heat the oil in a large skillet over medium heat. Add the chicken, in batches if necessary, and cook for 6 minutes on each side, or until golden brown and the juices run clear. Serve with the Sweet Potato Chutney. Garnish with mint sprigs, lemon slices, and jalapeño peppers.

SWEET-POTATO CHUTNEY

Combine 4 cups diced peeled sweet potatoes, 1 cup chopped onion, ¼ cup champagne vinegar, ¼ cup sugar, ⅓ cup dried cranberries, 3 tablespoons chopped crystallized ginger, 4 minced cloves garlic, 1 tablespoon curry powder, and ½ teaspoon salt in a large saucepan and bring to a boil over medium heat. Reduce the heat to low and cook, stirring frequently, for 30 minutes. Remove from the heat and stir in 3 tablespoons finely chopped fresh mint.

Makes 6 servings

Per serving: 768 calories, 38g protein, 58g carbohydrates, 44g fat, 5g saturated fat, 160mg cholesterol, 580mg sodium

SPICY STUFFED CHICKEN BREASTS

Prep **10 MINUTES**   *Cook/Bake* **46 MINUTES**

½   pound smoked sausage (andouille), thinly sliced

8   ounces white mushrooms, sliced

3   tablespoons chopped scallions

1   clove garlic, minced

1   tablespoon hot pepper sauce

4   tablespoons blue-cheese salad dressing

4   boneless, skinless chicken breast halves (about 1¼ pounds)

1   tablespoon Cajun seasoning

1⅓   cups long-grain white rice

Andouille, a spicy smoked sausage, can be hard to find outside of the South. If necessary, substitute a spicy kielbasa or a plain country smoked sausage.

LET'S BEGIN Cook the sausage in a large skillet over medium-high heat until it begins to brown. Add the mushrooms and sauté for 5 minutes. Add the scallions, garlic, and hot pepper sauce and sauté for 2 minutes. Transfer the mixture to a food processor and add 1 tablespoon of the salad dressing. Process until chopped. Cut 2-inch slits into the sides of the breasts and fill with as much stuffing as they will hold.

SEASON & SPICE Preheat the oven to 375°F. Sprinkle the chicken with the Cajun seasoning. Lightly oil a large skillet and set over medium-high heat until hot. Cook the chicken, turning once, for 5 minutes, or until brown.

INTO THE OVEN Cook the rice according to package directions and keep warm. Transfer the chicken to a lightly oiled 13x9-inch baking dish. Top with the leftover stuffing and drizzle with the remaining 3 tablespoons salad dressing. Bake for 30 minutes, or until the chicken juices run clear. Serve over the rice.

Makes 4 servings
Per serving: 667 calories, 47g protein, 54g carbohydrates, 28g fat, 8g saturated fat, 125mg cholesterol, 1,149mg sodium

EASY CHICKEN POT PIE

Prep **15 MINUTES**   *Bake* **8 MINUTES**

1   package (10 ounces)
    Italian-style carved
    cooked chicken breast

1   package (10 ounces)
    frozen mixed vegetables

1   can (10¾ ounces)
    condensed cream of
    potato soup

½   cup milk

10   refrigerated buttermilk
     biscuits

Pot pies usually take hours to make, but not this one! This one can be assembled fast on Saturday morning, then refrigerated for supper that night. Simply slide it into a hot oven and bake until bubbly.

LET'S BEGIN Preheat the oven to 450°F. Spray an 8-inch square baking dish with cooking spray. Cut the chicken into bite-size pieces. Combine the chicken, vegetables, soup, and milk in a large saucepan and bring to a simmer. Spoon into the prepared baking dish.

FIX IT FAST Starting in the center, place the biscuits on top of the chicken mixture in a single layer (don't worry if the biscuits do not reach all the way to the edge).

INTO THE OVEN Bake for 8 minutes, or until the biscuits puff and are brown.

Makes 4 servings

Per serving: 347 calories, 29g protein, 42g carbohydrate, 7g fat, 2g saturated fat, 68mg cholesterol, 1,149mg sodium

TOMATO-TOPPED CHICKEN & STUFFING

Prep **10 MINUTES**   *Bake* **30 MINUTES**

Stuffing cubes speed up the mixing and double as a "bed" and a topping for this chicken bake. Freshen up the flavors with a sprinkle of snipped chives or chopped parsley just before serving.

5	cups herb-seasoned stuffing cubes
6	tablespoons butter or margarine, melted
1¼	cups boiling water
4	chicken breast halves (about 2 pounds), boned and skin left on (1½ pounds)
1	can (10¾ ounces) condensed cream of chicken soup
⅓	cup milk
1	medium tomato, sliced

LET'S BEGIN Preheat the oven to 400°F. Crush 1 cup of the stuffing cubes and toss with 2 tablespoons of the butter in a medium bowl. Reserve for the topping.

TOSS IT Toss the remaining 4 cups stuffing cubes, the remaining 4 tablespoons butter, and the water together in a large bowl. Spoon into a 13x9-inch shallow baking dish. Place the chicken on top.

INTO THE OVEN Stir the soup and milk together until blended and pour over the chicken. Top with the tomato slices and sprinkle with the reserved topping. Bake for 30 minutes, or until the chicken juices run clear.

Makes 4 servings
Per serving: 738 calories, 40g protein, 55g carbohydrates, 40g fat, 17g saturated fat, 150mg cholesterol, 1,777mg sodium

---

Cooking Basics

SEASON UP FAST WITH STUFFING

Herb-seasoned stuffing cubes and mixes save at least a half hour of preparation time when stuffing the bird. But since they're already filled with seasonings, they can quickly spice up all kinds of chicken dishes. First turn a bag of seasoning cubes into crumbs by pulsing it in your food processor or blender. Now season away!

QUICK CHICKEN MAGIC
• Mix crumbs into chicken meatballs or chicken loaves.
• Coat chicken parts with Dijon mustard and sprinkle with seasoned crumbs. Then bake, grill. broil, or fry.
• Make your favorite Mac 'n' Cheese, stirring in chunks of cooked chicken. Sprinkle with crumbs, drizzle with melted butter, and bake as usual until bubbly.
• Toss crumbs with sautéed garlic and butter, sprinkle on chicken breasts, and bake.

FAST VEGETABLE MAGIC
• Stuff tomatoes with chopped cooked chicken, crumbs, and fresh snipped basil. Drizzle with oil and broil until golden.
• Stuff bell peppers with cooked ground chicken, sautéed onions, and crumbs. Sprinkle with shredded mozzarella and bake.

CHICKEN JAMBALAYA

Prep **20 MINUTES** *Cook* **45 MINUTES**

2	teaspoons canola oil
1	cup coarsely chopped andouille sausage
1	medium onion, chopped
1	rib celery, chopped
1	green bell pepper, chopped
6	boneless, skinless chicken thighs (about 1½ pounds), cut into 1-inch chunks
2	garlic cloves, minced
1	teaspoon chopped fresh thyme
1	teaspoon chopped fresh oregano
1	teaspoon salt
½	teaspoon ground black pepper
½	teaspoon ground red pepper
1	can (14 ounces) whole tomatoes
1	can (14 ounces) tomato sauce
2	cups chicken broth
4	scallions, chopped
1	cup long-grain white rice

Late one night at a New Orleans inn, the owner asked Chef Jean to "mix up some things together fast" for a late-night guest. He named it Jean Balayez, which later became jambalaya.

LET'S BEGIN Heat the oil in a large skillet over medium heat. Sauté the sausage for 8 minutes, or until crisp around the edge. Sauté the onion, celery, and bell pepper for 5 minutes, or until soft. Increase the heat to medium-high and add the chicken. Sauté for 8 minutes, or until light brown. Reduce the heat to medium, stir in the garlic, thyme, oregano, salt, black pepper, and red pepper, and sauté for 3 minutes longer.

SIMMER LOW Stir in the tomatoes with their juice, the tomato sauce, broth, scallions and rice. Bring to a simmer, then reduce the heat to very low. Cover and cook for 20 minutes, or until the rice absorbs the liquid. Serve.

Makes 4 servings

Per serving: 613 calories, 37g protein, 55g carbohydrates, 24g fat, 8g saturated fat, 126mg cholesterol, 2,422mg sodium

---

Food Facts

LOVE THOSE LEGS & THIGHS!

Based on price-per-pound, leg quarters are the least expensive cut of chicken. Buy them on sale and stock up the freezer.

How does dark meat get its color? From myoglobin, a protein that retains oxygen in (well-used) muscles.

A perfect match! Chicken legs and thighs are ideal for the grill.

Dark meat is full of collagen, which melts into the meat as it grills, making them extra juicy.

Nutritionally, drums are great. According to the American Dietetic Association, 3 ounces of a baked chicken drumstick (skin removed) has less total fat than 3 ounces of pork chop, sirloin steak, beef tenderloin, or salmon.

COMPANY CORNISH HENS

Prep **10 MINUTES** *Roast* **50 MINUTES**

These hybrids of Cornish and White Rock chickens are actually miniature little chicks that weigh in around 2 pounds (2½ pounds tops). They're a made-to-order company dinner, because they cook faster than a whole bird.

1	medium eggplant, chopped
1	medium zucchini, chopped
1	can (14½ ounces) diced tomatoes seasoned with green pepper and onion
½	cup olive-oil vinaigrette (either store-bought or homemade)
8	fresh oregano sprigs
2	fresh Cornish game hens (1¾ pounds each)

MIX IT UP Preheat the oven to 350°F. Place the eggplant, zucchini, and tomatoes and their juices in a large bowl. Pour the vinaigrette over the mixture and gently stir to coat. Set aside.

SEASON & SPICE Remove the giblets from the hens and discard. Gently loosen the skin from the birds and tuck the oregano into these pockets. Place the hens in a roasting pan and surround with the vegetables.

INTO THE OVEN Roast the hens for 50 to 60 minutes, or until a meat thermometer inserted in thickest part of the thigh (not touching any bone) reads 170° F.

Makes 4 servings

Per serving: 394 calories, 32g protein, 13g carbohydrates, 24g fat, 7g saturated fat, 170mg cholesterol, 358mg sodium

Food Facts

CORNISH HENS—A NUTRITIOUS DISH
These Company Cornish Hens are great tasting and pretty enough for any special dinner party. But our recipe is also chock full of things good for you!

LOADED WITH MINERALS
A 3-ounce portion of Cornish game hen provides 25% of the Daily Value for the mineral selenium, which may play a role in preventing some types of cancer and heart disease.

TOMATOES
Eat tomatoes and you may be decreasing your risk of heart disease and cancer. They contain lycopene—the compound that gives tomatoes their red color. Lycopene helps protect your body cells from the destructive effects of "free radicals" that have been linked to heart disease and some forms of cancer.

HEALTHY OLIVE OIL
It's no secret—olive oil is a fat that's good for your heart. It has a rich amount of monounsaturated fat that helps lower LDLs ("bad" cholesterol). People following the Mediterranean diet, which contains a lot of olive oil, have been found to have less heart disease than those on typical American diets.

CHICKEN-HERB QUICHE SQUARES

Prep **15 MINUTES**   Bake **30 MINUTES**

1	tube (10 ounces) refrigerated pizza crust
1	package (6 ounces) grilled chicken breast strips
1	large tomato, chopped
½	cup chopped green bell pepper
½	cup chopped onion
¼	cup grated Parmesan cheese
4	large eggs
3	tablespoons water
½	teaspoon dried Italian seasoning

Quiches are great served either room temperature or hot from the oven. Make this quiche creamier by using half-and-half for water.

LET'S BEGIN Preheat the oven to 375°F. Butter a 13x9-inch baking dish. Press the pizza crust dough onto the bottom and halfway up the sides of the dish.

LAYER Top the crust with the chicken, tomato, bell pepper, and onion. Sprinkle with the Parmesan.

INTO THE OVEN Whisk the eggs, water, and Italian seasoning together in a bowl until light and frothy. Pour over the vegetables. Bake the pizza for 30 minutes, or until the center puffs up and the edges are set. Let stand 5 minutes before cutting.

Makes 6 to 8 servings

Per serving: 244 calories, 19g protein, 25g carbohydrates, 7g fat, 2g saturated fat, 168mg cholesterol, 387mg sodium

SuperQuick
BROILED CHICKEN MAGIC

Prep **5 MINUTES**   Broil **25 MINUTES**

1	chicken, quartered (about 3 pounds), skin removed from all but the wings
1	teaspoon salt
½	teaspoon ground black pepper
½	teaspoon ground thyme
2	tablespoons butter or margarine, cut into pieces
¼	cup lemon juice
4	teaspoons turbinado crystalline sugar

Turbinado sugar has been "steam-cleaned," leaving bronze-color crystals with a delicate molasses flavor. It glazes dishes fast!

LET'S BEGIN Rinse the chicken and pat dry. Mix the salt, pepper, and thyme together and rub all over the chicken.

BROIL IT HOT Preheat the broiler. Oil broiler pan and arrange chicken, bone side down. Dot with butter. Broil the chicken 5 inches from heat, turning twice, for 20 minutes. Drizzle with lemon juice and sprinkle with sugar. Broil for 5 minutes longer, or until golden brown and the juices run clear.

Makes 4 servings

Per serving: 270 calories, 35g protein, 6g carbohydrates, 11g fat, 5g saturated fat, 131mg cholesterol, 771mg sodium

Chicken-Herb Quiche Squares

CHICKEN-TACO CORN BREAD PIE

Prep **15 MINUTES**   *Cook/Bake* **38 MINUTES**

1½	pounds boneless, skinless chicken breast halves
1	tablespoon vegetable oil
1	package (1¼ ounces) taco seasoning mix
1	green bell pepper, chopped
¾	cup water
1	cup shredded Cheddar cheese (4 ounces)
1	package (8½ ounces) corn muffin mix

Here's a taco pie that's ready in half the time of the original.

LET'S BEGIN Preheat the oven to 400°F. Cut the chicken into 1-inch chunks. Sauté in oil in a large skillet over medium-high heat for 8 minutes. Drain off the fat. Add seasoning mix, bell pepper, and water and bring to a boil. Reduce the heat. Simmer, stirring, for 10 minutes. Spoon into 9-inch pie plate.

LAYER & BAKE Sprinkle pie with Cheddar. Prepare muffin mix per package directions and spoon on top. Bake for 20 minutes, or until golden brown. Let stand for 5 minutes.

> **Makes 4 to 6 servings**
>
> *Per serving: 620 calories, 51g protein, 51g carbohydrates, 22g fat, 9g saturated fat, 130mg cholesterol, 1,766 mg sodium*

SuperQuick

CREAMY TARRAGON CHICKEN

Prep **10 MINUTES**   *Cook* **20 MINUTES**

1	package (6 ounces) garlic-butter rice
1½	cups all-purpose flour
	Salt and ground black pepper
6	chicken breast halves, (about 2¼ pounds), bone removed and skin left on
2	tablespoons olive oil
1	cup chicken broth
1	cup milk
2	teaspoons dried tarragon

Fresh tarragon is sweet and strong, with an aniselike flavor. It quickly perfumes this creamy sauce.

LET'S BEGIN Prepare the rice according to package directions and keep warm. Mix the flour, salt, and pepper on waxed paper and coat the chicken, saving the extra flour.

INTO THE PAN Heat the oil in a large skillet over medium-high heat. Cook the chicken, turning once, for 8 minutes, or until brown. Transfer to a plate.

MAKE IT SAUCY Whisk 1 tablespoon of the flour into oil. Whisk in the broth, milk, and tarragon. Return the chicken to the skillet. Cover and simmer for 5 minutes. Serve over rice.

> **Makes 6 servings**
>
> *Per serving: 533 calories, 38g protein, 47g carbohydrates, 21g fat, 5g saturated fat, 99mg cholesterol, 716mg sodium*

EASY HOME-STYLE CHICKEN
Prep **4 MINUTES**   *Bake* **26 MINUTES**

Buttermilk baking mix and honey are the magical partners in this easy oven-baked chicken. Feel free to substitute a cut-up whole chicken or chicken parts.

½	cup honey
½	cup buttermilk baking mix
2	teaspoons ground ginger
1	teaspoon seasoned salt
¼	teaspoon ground black pepper
4	boneless, skinless chicken breast halves (about 1¼ pounds)
2	tablespoons vegetable oil

LET'S BEGIN Preheat the oven to 350°F. Pour the honey into a pie plate. Mix the baking mix, ginger, seasoned salt, and pepper together in a separate pie plate. Coat the chicken with the honey, then coat with the seasoned baking mix, gently patting so the crumbs adhere.

INTO THE PAN Heat the oil in a large nonstick skillet over medium-high heat. Cook the chicken, turning once, for 6 minutes, or until golden brown. Drain off the oil.

BAKE Place the chicken on a rack set in a roasting pan and bake for 20 to 30 minutes, until the juices run clear.

Makes 4 servings
Per serving: 412 calories, 34g protein, 45g carbohydrates, 11g fat, 2g saturated fat, 82mg cholesterol, 660mg sodium

---

Time Saver

15-MINUTE CHICKEN STOCKS

MAKE THE MOST OF A CAN
Turn a can (or several cans) of chicken broth into your own homemade one by simmering it for 15 minutes (instead of the traditional 3 hours) with one or more of these ingredients:
• a sliced carrot and celery rib
• a dried bay leaf
• a small sliced onion studded with whole cloves
• a few peppercorns
• 2 to 4 sprigs of thyme
• a chopped, seeded tomato
• a few cloves of garlic
After the simmer, strain and refrigerate. Use this fast-made stock in any recipe calling for chicken stock.

MAKE IT ETHNIC!
Let your canned broth travel the world (still takes only 15 minutes)!
Chinese Add a slice of fresh gingerroot, a smashed garlic clove, a sliced scallion.
Mexican Boot up the flavor with chili powder, sliced scallions, plus dried thyme and cilantro.
French Toss in fresh tarragon, a garlic clove, some chives.
Italian Stir in a garlic clove and some Italian seasoning.
Thai Spice it up with ginger, lemongrass, and shallots.

TORTILLA-CRUSTED CHICKEN PAILLARD

Prep **14 MINUTES**   *Cook* **16 MINUTES**

4   boneless, skinless
       chicken breast halves
       (about 1¼ pounds)

¼   cup all-purpose flour

2   cups tortilla chips,
       finely crushed

1   large egg white

1   tablespoon water

2   teaspoons vegetable oil

Sacaton Relish (see recipe)

Crush the tortilla chips fast in a food processor or blender by pulsing the blade. Or place the chips in a resealable plastic bag, push out the air, and seal. Roll over them with a rolling pin.

LET'S BEGIN Place the chicken breasts between plastic wrap and pound until ¼ inch thick. Put the flour and tortilla crumbs on separate sheets of waxed paper. Whisk the egg white and water together in a pie plate. Coat each piece of chicken with the flour, shaking off the excess, dip into the egg, and then into the crumbs to coat evenly.

COOK IT QUICK Heat the oil in a large nonstick skillet over medium-high heat. Cook the chicken, turning once, for 6 minutes, or until brown. Reduce the heat to medium-low and cook the chicken for 10 minutes longer, or until the juices run clear. Prepare relish while chicken simmers. To serve, place the chicken on a platter and spoon the warm relish on top.

SACATON RELISH

Cook 3 slices bacon in a large skillet over medium-low heat just until crisp. Add 1 medium chopped onion and cook until softened, about 6 minutes. Stir in 2 medium chopped tomatoes, 1 can (4½ ounces) drained chopped mild green chilies, ¼ teaspoon salt and ¼ teaspoon ground black pepper. Cook for 3 minutes. Transfer to a serving dish and keep warm.

Makes 4 servings
Per serving: 391 calories, 37g protein, 29g carbohydrates, 15g fat, 2g saturated fat, 88mg cholesterol, 560mg sodium

CREDITS

PAGE 2 California Table Grape Commission: Photo for Chicken Véronique courtesy of California Table Grape Commission. Used with permission.

PAGE 8 National Chicken Council: Photo for Tortilla-crusted Chicken Paillard courtesy of the National Chicken Council/U.S. Poultry & Egg Association. Used with permission.

PAGE 18 Maille: Recipe for Chicken with Old-Style Dijon Mustard Sauce courtesy of Maille. Used with permission.

PAGE 19 French's: Recipe and photo for Savory Lemon Chicken Skillet courtesy of *French's* French Fried Onions. Used with permission.

PAGE 20 McIlhenny Company: Recipe for California Lime Chicken courtesy of McIlhenny Company. Used with permission.

PAGE 21 Ocean Spray Cranberries: Recipe and photo for Apple-Cranberry Chicken Marsala courtesy of Ocean Spray Cranberries, Inc. Used with permission.

PAGE 22 USA Rice Federation: Recipe for Chicken & Rice l'Orange courtesy of USA Rice Federation. Used with permission.

PAGES 22/23 Kraft Foods: Recipe and photo for Quick Chicken Stir-fry courtesy of Kraft Kitchens. Used with permission.

PAGE 24 California Table Grape Commission: Recipe for Chicken Véronique courtesy of California Table Grape Commission. Used with permission.

PAGE 25 Welch's: Recipe for Concord Sizzle courtesy of Welch's. Used with permission.

PAGE 26 Uncle Ben's: Lemon-Olive Chicken with Wild Rice courtesy of UNCLE BEN'S® Brand. Used with permission.

PAGES 26/27 Kraft Foods: Recipe and Photo for Linguine Primavera Parmesan courtesy of Kraft Kitchens. Used with permission.

PAGE 28 McIlhenny Company: Recipe for Spanish Holiday courtesy of McIlhenny Company. Used with permission.

PAGE 29 National Honey Board: Recipe for Quick Honey Fried Chicken courtesy of the National Honey Board. Used with permission.

PAGES 30/31 Jenny Craig: Recipe and photo for Breast of Chicken Balsamic courtesy of Jenny Craig, Inc. Used with permission.

PAGE 32 Del Monte: Recipe and photo for Pick of the Garden courtesy of Del Monte Foods. Used with permission.

PAGE 33 Birds Eye: Recipe for Chicken-Vegetable Teriyaki courtesy of Birds Eye Foods. Used with permission.

PAGE 34 Tone Brothers: Recipe for Sweet & Spicy Stir-fry courtesy of Tone Brothers, Inc., producer of Tone's, Spice Islands, and Durkee products. Used with permission.

PAGES 34/35 Kraft Foods: Recipe and photo for Mediterranean Chicken Breasts courtesy of Kraft Kitchens. Used with permission.

PAGE 36 Land O'Lakes: Recipe and photo for Tenders with Lemon-Spinach Rice courtesy of Land O'Lakes, Inc. Used with permission.

PAGE 37 8th Continent: Recipe for Chicken with Dijon Crème courtesy of 8th Continent, LLC. 8TH CONTINENT® trademark used with permission.

PAGE 38 USA Rice Federation: Recipe and photo for Chicken Romano courtesy of USA Rice Federation. Used with permission.

PAGE 39 McIlhenny Company: Recipe for Chicken in Brandied Cream courtesy of McIlhenny Company. Used with permission.

PAGE 40 Kraft Foods: Photo for Stir-fry Salad courtesy of Kraft Kitchens. Used with permission.

PAGE 42 Hormel: Recipe for Easy Caesar Salad courtesy of Hormel Foods. Used with permission.

PAGES 42/43 National Chicken Council: Recipe and photo for Chicken Waldorf Salad courtesy of the National Chicken Council/U.S. Poultry & Egg Association. Used with permission.

PAGE 44 Kraft Foods: Recipe for Southwestern Grilled Salad courtesy of Kraft Kitchens. Used with permission.

PAGE 44 Kraft Foods: Recipe and photo for Honey-Mustard Chicken Salad courtesy of Kraft Kitchens. Used with permission.

PAGE 45 California Strawberry Commission: Recipe for Strawberry-Patch Salad courtesy of the © California Strawberry Commission. All rights reserved. Used with permission.

PAGES 46/47 Kraft Foods: Recipe and photo for Chicken Antipasto Salad courtesy of Kraft Kitchens. Used with permission.

PAGE 47 Kraft Foods: Recipe for Stir-fry Salad courtesy of Kraft Kitchens. Used with permission.

PAGES 48/49 Dole: Recipe and photo for Chicken, Broccoli, & Pineapple Stir-fry courtesy of Dole Food Company. Used with permission.

PAGE 50 Holland House: Recipe for Chicken Primavera courtesy of Holland House. Used with permission.

PAGE 51 Perdue: Recipe and photo for Asian Coleslaw courtesy of © Perdue Farms. Used with permission.

PAGES 52/53 Sunkist: Recipe and photo for Grilled Chicken, Grapefruit, & Arugula Salad courtesy of Sunkist Growers, Inc. Used with permission.

PAGES 54/55 California Walnut Marketing Board: Recipe and photo for Asian Walnut Chicken courtesy of The California Walnut Marketing Board. Used with permission.

PAGE 56 Perdue: Recipe and photo for Fusion Stir-fry courtesy of © Perdue Farms. Used with permission.

PAGE 57 Perdue: Recipe for Orange-Teriyaki Stir-fry courtesy of © Perdue Farms. Used with permission.

PAGES 58/59 McIlhenny Company: Recipe and photo for Chicken & Black Bean Salad courtesy of McIlhenny Company. Used with permission.

PAGES 60/61 Association for Dressings & Sauces: Recipe and photo for Wisconsin Cheese & Grilled Chicken Salad courtesy of The Association for Dressings and Sauces. Used with permission.

PAGE 62 National Chicken Council: Photo for Chicken Tacos with Corn Salsa courtesy of the National Chicken Council/U.S. Poultry & Egg Association. Used with permission.

PAGE 64 Cherry Marketing Institute: Recipe and photo for Cherry-Chicken Croissants courtesy of The Cherry Marketing Institute. Used with permission.

PAGE 65 California Walnut Marketing Board: Recipe for Open-Faced Sandwiches with Orange-Walnut Mayonnaise courtesy of The California Walnut Marketing Board. Used with permission.

PAGE 66 McIlhenny Company: Recipe for Chicken & Pepper Heroes courtesy of McIlhenny Company. Used with permission.

PAGES 66/67 Kraft Foods: Recipe and photo for Garden Salad Sub courtesy of Kraft Kitchens. Used with permission.

PAGE 68 Pillsbury: Recipe for Cheesy Chicken Biscuit Sandwiches provided courtesy of The Pillsbury Company, a subsidiary of General mills, Inc. Used with permission.

PAGE 69 National Chicken Council: Recipe and photo for Barbecue & Slaw Buns courtesy of the National Chicken Council/U.S. Poultry & Egg Association. Used with permission.

PAGE 70 National Chicken Council: Recipe and photo for Pita Pockets courtesy of the National Chicken Council/ U.S. Poultry & Egg Association. Used with permission.

PAGE 71 McCormick: Recipe for Grilled Cheesy Chicken Pockets courtesy of McCormick's. Used with permission.

PAGE 71 Perdue: Recipe for Tex-Mex Enchiladas courtesy of © Perdue Farms. Used with permission.

PAGE 72 Campbell Soup Company: Recipe for Cheesy Chicken Pizza courtesy of Campbell Soup Company. Used with permission.

PAGES 72/73 Perdue: Recipe and photo for Pizza Santa Fe courtesy of © Perdue Farms. Used with permission.

PAGES 74/75 Wisconsin Milk Marketing Board: Recipe and photo for Ranch Pizza Pie courtesy of the Wisconsin Milk Marketing Board, Inc. Used with permission.

PAGE 75 Boboli: Recipe for 20-Minute Pizza courtesy of Entenmann's Products, Inc. Used with permission.

PAGE 76 Kraft Foods: Recipe for Honey-of-a-Wrap courtesy of Kraft Kitchens. Used with permission.

PAGES 76/77 McIlhenny Company: Recipe and photo for Chicken & Avocado Wraps courtesy of McIlhenny Company. Used with permission.

PAGE 78 Wish-Bone®: Recipe for Chicken Ranch Wraps courtesy of Wish-Bone®. Used with permission.

PAGE 79 National Chicken Council: Recipe for Chicken Tacos with Corn Salsa courtesy of the National Chicken Council/ U.S. Poultry & Egg Association. Used with permission.

PAGE 80 National Chicken Council: Photo for Easy Chicken Stroganoff courtesy of the National Chicken Council/ U.S. Poultry & Egg Association. Used with permission.

PAGES 82/83 National Chicken Council: Recipe and photo for Skillet Italiano courtesy of the National Chicken Council/U.S. Poultry & Egg Association. Used with permission.

PAGES 84/85 National Chicken Council: Recipe and photo for Spaghetti & Meatballs courtesy of the National Chicken Council/U.S. Poultry & Egg Association. Used with permission.

PAGE 86 Uncle Ben's: Recipe for Rice-Stuffed Poblano Chilies courtesy of UNCLE BEN'S® Brand. Used with permission.

PAGE 87 Uncle Ben's: Recipe for Gumbo on the Bayou courtesy of UNCLE BEN'S® Brand. Used with permission.

PAGES 88/89 Perdue: Recipe and photo for Pennsylvania Dutch Chicken Bake courtesy of © Perdue Farms. Used with permission.

PAGE 89 U.S. Apple Association: Recipe for Oriental Stir-fry courtesy of the U.S. Apple Association. Used with permission.

PAGES 90/91 Kikkoman: Recipe and photo for Teriyaki Rice Bowl courtesy of Kikkoman. Used with permission.

PAGES 92/93 USA Rice Federation: Recipe and photo for Spiced-Up Thai Salad courtesy of USA Rice Federation. Used with permission.

PAGE 94 Uncle Ben's: Recipe for Chicken & Macadamia Fried Rice courtesy of UNCLE BEN'S® Brand. Used with permission.

PAGE 95 Birds Eye: Recipe for Chicken Cacciatore courtesy of Birds Eye Foods. Used with permission.

PAGES 96/97 California Walnut Marketing Board: Recipe and photo for Walnut Chicken for a Crowd courtesy of The California Walnut Marketing Board. Used with permission.

PAGE 97 Kraft Foods: Recipe for 15-Minute Tacos courtesy of Kraft Kitchens. Used with permission.

PAGE 98 National Chicken Council: Recipe and photo for Chicken Schnitzel with Lemon courtesy of the National Chicken Council/U.S. Poultry & Egg Association. Used with permission.

PAGE 99 National Chicken Council: Recipe for Easy Chicken Stroganoff courtesy of the National Chicken Council/ U.S. Poultry & Egg Association. Used with permission.

PAGE 100 Kraft Foods & Reynold Wrap: Photo for Barbecue Packets courtesy of Kraft Kitchens and Reynold Wrap Heavy Duty Aluminum Foil. Used with permission.

WEBSITES

PAGE 102 Dole: Recipe and photo for Easy Barbecue Kabobs courtesy of Dole Food Company. Used with permission.

PAGE 103 French's: Recipe and photo for North Carolina Barbecue courtesy of French's® mustard and Frank's® RedHot® Cayenne Pepper Sauce. Used with permission.

PAGES 104/105 McIlhenny Company: Recipe and photo for Thai Skewers courtesy of McIlhenny Company. Used with permission.

PAGES 106/107 French's: Recipe and photo for Grilled Chicken Satay courtesy of French's® mustard, French's® Worcestershire Sauce and Frank's® RedHot® Cayenne Pepper Sauce. Used with permission.

PAGE 108 Kraft Foods: Recipe and photo for BBQ & Grilled Vegetables courtesy of Kraft Kitchens. Used with permission.

PAGE 109 McIlhenny Company: Recipe for Surf 'n' Turf Grill courtesy of McIlhenny Company. Used with permission.

PAGE 110 Kraft Foods & Reynold Wrap: Recipe for Barbecue Packets courtesy of Kraft Kitchens and Reynold Wrap Heavy Duty Aluminum Foil. Used with permission.

PAGE 110 Welch's: Recipe for Ginger-glazed Cutlets courtesy of Welch's. Used with permission.

PAGE 111 National Chicken Council: Recipe for Chicken with Grape Salsa courtesy of the National Chicken Council/U.S. Poultry & Egg Association. Used with permission.

PAGE 112 Colavita: Recipe for Outdoor Grill with Fresh Herbs courtesy of Colavita. Used with permission.

PAGE 113 French's: Recipe and photo for Rosemary Chicken courtesy of French's® mustard. Used with permission.

PAGE 114 National Honey Board: Recipe for West Coast Barbecued Chicken courtesy of the National Honey Board. Used with permission.

PAGES 114/115 Mott's: Recipe and photo for Grilled Lemon Chicken Dijon courtesy of Holland House. Used with permission.

PAGE 116 National Chicken Council: Photo for Sweet & Tart Chicken Roast courtesy of the National Chicken Council/U.S. Poultry & Egg Association. Used with permission.

PAGES 118/119 Perdue: Recipe and photo for Easy Sunday Dinner courtesy of © Perdue Farms. Used with permission.

PAGE 120 McIlhenny Company: Recipe for Crisp & Crunchy Oven Fry courtesy of McIlhenny Company. Used with permission.

PAGES 120/121 National Chicken Council: Recipe and photo for Devilish Chicken courtesy of the National Chicken Council/U.S. Poultry & Egg Association. Used with permission.

PAGE 121 National Chicken Council: Recipe for Sweet & Tart Chicken Roast courtesy of the National Chicken Council/U.S. Poultry & Egg Association. Used with permission.

PAGES 122/123 Mott's: Recipe and photo for Lemon–Herb Roast Chicken courtesy of Holland House. Used with permission.

PAGES 124/125 Cherry Marketing Institute: Recipe and photo for Cherry-glazed Chicken courtesy of The Cherry Marketing Institute. Used

PAGE 125 Mott's: Recipe for Mandarin Orange Chicken courtesy of Holland House. Used with permission.

PAGE 126 National Chicken Council: Recipe for Pecan-crusted Chicken with Sweet-Potato Chutney courtesy of the National Chicken Council/U.S. Poultry & Egg Association. Used with permission.

PAGE 127 Bruce Foods: Recipe for Spicy Stuffed Chicken Breasts courtesy of Bruce Foods Corporation. Used with permission.

PAGE 128 Perdue: Recipe and photo for Easy Chicken Pot Pie courtesy of © Perdue Farms. Used with permission.

PAGE 129 Campbell Soup Company: Recipe for Tomato-topped Chicken & Stuffing courtesy of Campbell Soup Company. Used with permission.

PAGES 130/131 National Chicken Council: Recipe and photo for Chicken Jambalaya courtesy of the National Chicken Council/U.S. Poultry & Egg Association. Used with permission.

PAGES 132/133 Perdue: Recipe and photo for Company Cornish Hens courtesy of © Perdue Farms. Used with permission.

PAGE 134 Sugar In The Raw: Recipe for Broiled Chicken Magic courtesy of Sugar In The Raw®, a registered trademark of Cumberland Packing Corporation. Used with permission.

PAGES 134/135 Kraft Foods: Recipe and photo for Chicken-Herb Quiche Squares courtesy of Kraft Kitchens. Used with permission.

PAGE 136 Kraft Foods: Recipe for Chicken-Taco Corn Bread Pie courtesy of Kraft Kitchens. Used with permission.

PAGE 136 Uncle Ben's: Recipe for Creamy Tarragon Chicken: courtesy of UNCLE BEN'S® Brand. Used with permission.

PAGE 137 National Honey Board: Recipe for Easy Home-style Chicken courtesy of the National Honey Board. Used with permission.

PAGES 138/139 National Chicken Council: Recipe and photo for Tortilla-crusted Chicken Paillard courtesy of the National Chicken Council/U.S. Poultry & Egg Association. Used with permission.

RODALE INC.
www.rodale.com

Association of Dressings & Sauces
www.dressings-sauces.org

Birds Eye Foods
www.birdseyefoods.com

Bruce Foods Corporation
www.brucefoods.com

California Strawberry Commission
www.calstrawberry.com

California Table Grape Commission
www.freshCaliforniagrapes.com

California Walnut Marketing Board
www.walnuts.org

Campbell Soup Company
www.campbellkitchen.com

Cherry Marketing Institute
www.usacherries.com

Colavita
www.colavita.com

Del Monte Foods
www.delmonte.com

Dole Food Company
www.dole.com

8th Continent
www.8thcontinent.com

French's
www.frenchsfoods.com

Holland House
www.cooking wine.com

Hormel Foods
www.hormel.com

Jenny Craig
www.jennycraig.com

Kikkoman
www.kikkoman-usa.com

Kraft Foods
www.kraftfoods.com

Land O'Lakes
www.landolakes.com

Maille
www.maille.com

McCormick
www.mccormick.com

McIlhenny Company
www.tabasco.com

National Chicken Council
www.eatchicken.com

National Honey Board
www.honey.com

Ocean Spray Cranberries
www.oceanspray.com

Perdue Farms
www.perdue.com

Pillsbury
www.pillsbury.com

Sugar in the Raw
www.sugarintheraw.com

Sunkist
www.sunkist.com

Tone Brothers
www.spiceadvice.com

Uncle Ben's
www.unclebens.com

U.S. Apple Association
www.usapple.org

USA Rice Federation
www.ricecafe.com

Welch's
www.welchs.com

Wisconsin Milk Marketing Board
www.wisdairy.com

Wish-Bone
www.wish-bone.com

INDEX

✔ Designates a SuperQuick recipe that gets you in and out of the kitchen in 30 minutes or less!
Bold faced page numbers refer to photographs.